BASIC ANTHROPOLOGY UNITS

GENERAL EDITORS

George and Louise Spindler

STANFORD UNIVERSITY

VARIATION IN KINSHIP

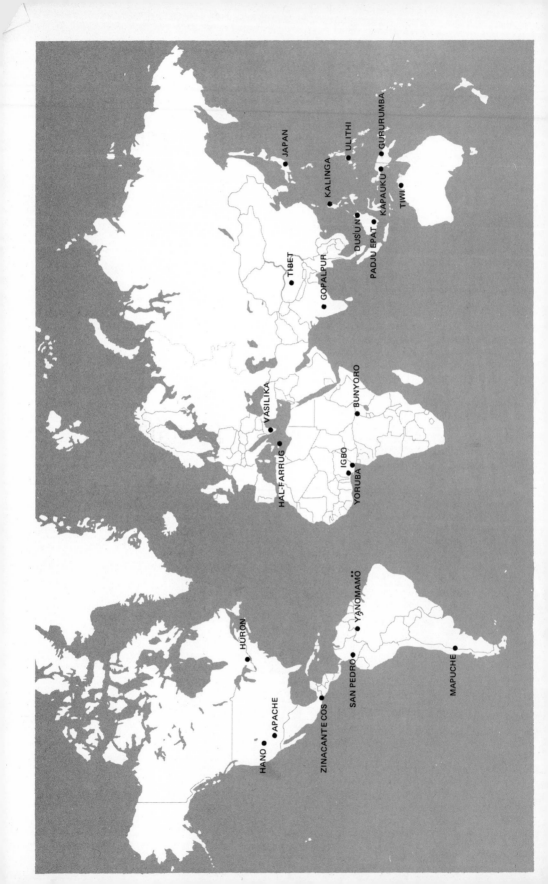

ERNEST L. SCHUSKY
Southern Illinois University

Variation in Kinship

HOLT, RINEHART AND WINSTON, INC.
New York   Chicago   San Francisco   Atlanta
Dallas   Montreal   Toronto   London   Sydney

Library of Congress Cataloging in Publication Data

Schusky, Ernest Lester, 1931–
        Variation in kinship.

        (Basic anthropology units)
        Bibliography: p. 71
        1. Kinship.   I. Title.
GN480.S36   301.42'1   73–7898
        ISBN: 0–03–091312–8

Foreword

THE BASIC ANTHROPOLOGY UNITS

Basic Anthropology Units are designed to introduce students to essential topics in the contemporary study of man. In combination they have greater depth and scope than any single textbook. They may also be assigned selectively to cover topics relevant to the particular profile of a given course, or they may be utilized separately as authoritative guides to significant aspects of anthropology.

Many of the Basic Anthropology Units serve as the point of intellectual departure from which to draw on the Case Studies in Cultural Anthropology and Case Studies in Education and Culture. This integration is designed to enable instructors to utilize these easily available materials for their instructional purposes. The combination introduces flexibility and innovation in teaching and avoids the constraints imposed by the encyclopedic textbook. To this end, selected Case Studies have been annotated in each unit. Questions and exercises have also been provided as suggestive leads for instructors and students toward productive engagements with ideas and data in other sources as well as the Case Studies.

This series was planned over a period of several years by a number of anthropologists, some of whom are authors of the separate Basic Units. The completed series will include units representing all the basic sectors of contemporary anthropology, including archeology, biological anthropology, and linguistics, as well as the various subfields of social and cultural anthropology.

THE AUTHOR

Ernest Schusky began graduate work in 1952 at the University of Arizona, where his first fieldwork was among Papago Indians. In 1960 he completed his PhD at the University of Chicago after fieldwork among the Lower Brule Dakota.

In the summer of 1964 he studied in India as a Fulbright Scholar; in 1966–1967 he was a postdoctoral student at the London School of Economics. Since 1960 he has been at Southern Illinois University, Edwardsville, where he currently is Professor and Chairman of Anthropology.

With Patrick Culbert he is the author of *Introducing Culture*. His other books are *Manual for Kinship Analysis* and *The Right To Be Indian*. He has also published on Dakota demography, politics, religion, and economic development.

THIS UNIT

This introduction to one of the most important topics in anthropology is straightforward, understandable, and has the great virtue of being related to a number of Case Studies. Generalizations about kinship, kin groups, descent, and affinity are illustrated by showing how they apply to specific groups and the behavior of people in them. Often the author uses the case inductively, starting with a demarcation of an area of behavior, presenting the data, and then arriving at generalizations as the case is explored. This strategy helps remove some of the abstraction that often obscures the study of kinship for the beginning student.

For the reader who wants to learn more about kinship there are scores of articles and books at different levels of sophistication and complexity. In this unit, an introduction to these sources can be found at the end of each chapter, and many others are referenced in the bibliography. A very useful extension of the core concepts found in this Basic Anthropology Unit is contained in Dr. Schusky's *Manual for Kinship Analysis* (1972).

George and Louise Spindler
General Editors
STANFORD, CALIF.

Contents

CONTENTS

1
The Nature of Kinship

Anthropologists have been studying the kinship systems of people all over the world for more than a century. At first, great differences in the ways various people named relatives and behaved toward them attracted our attention, but we soon discovered that similarities in kinship practices were even more fascinating than the differences.

Beginning students of anthropology are generally more intrigued with the differences because systems of kinship are learned early in life with little or no explanation. That is, you learned who your uncles and aunts were long before you learned any principle that parents' siblings and their spouses equaled uncle and aunt. Your kinship system seems "only natural" to you, and it will come as a surprise to you that elsewhere it is "natural" to have eight or ten "fathers" and "mothers" or that the mother's brother is a type of relative entirely different from father's brother. Once you see that these two men can be different types, it should be obvious that a mother's brother's daughter is quite a different relative from a father's brother's daughter, even though both are simply "first cousins" in your way of thinking.

A simple problem can illustrate the potential differences between the two men that English speakers classify together as "uncle." If your father were to die, which of your uncles might your mother marry? She is not likely to marry either of them, but she will never marry any of those who are her brothers. However, she could marry any of your father's brothers. After all, they are likely to be somewhat like your father; your mother knows them and you know them. The second marriage would not create new in-law relationships but simply reaffirm old ones. Such marriages have advantages, and many peoples make a practice of marrying the siblings of deceased spouses. The point here is that it clearly makes sense to treat the mother's brother as an entirely different type of relative from father's brother. Our practice is a bit "unnatural" in that we group these two relatives together; that is, we put them into the same status or category just as we group their children together in the one status of "cousin."

Speaking of cousins, we might further inquire into the nature of kinship by asking what is a cousin. You have probably never asked yourself the question before but are assured you know what one is. Before going further, take a guess at how many different "types" of relatives make up the status of first cousin and how many different "types" of second cousins there are. Now write out a list of

1

first cousins such as: mother's brother's daughter, mother's brother's son, mother's sister's daughter, and so on. Useful abbreviations are M (mother), F (father), B (brother), Z (sister), D (daughter), S (son), H (husband), and W (wife). Anthropologists designate these eight words as *primary kin terms*; they alone are sufficient to describe all the types of kinship relations.

Your list of first cousins should have eight types: MBD, MBS, BZD, MZS, FBD, FBS, FZD, FZS. How many second cousins are there?

CONSANGUINEAL KINSHIP

A more important question is how are all these relationships traced. The answer suggests the nature of the kinship link. The primary kin through whom you "reach" a cousin are what we call "blood" relatives. Anthropologists call them *consanguineal* relatives, and their ties are all based on *descent*, that is, a parent to child link. Your brother is related to you because he is your father's son or your mother's son. Likewise, mother's sister is really mother's mother's daughter, but we simplify the relationship to "mother's sister." The point is that all of these consanguineal relationships rest on descent ties.

The descent ties are more vividly demonstrated through kinship diagrams. Whereas kinship terms often blur distinctions, a diagram is always specific. Anthropologists use a method of diagramming kin relations similar to one that geneticists use. A triangle represents a male, a circle a female. Differences in generation are specified by levels. A sibling tie is indicated by a horizontal line over symbols; descent by a vertical line; and marriage by a horizontal line under symbols. A husband and wife with two children are diagrammed in Figure 1A. A husband and two wives with their children are shown in Figure 1B.

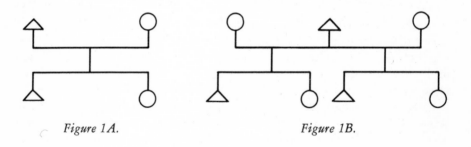

Figure 1A.   Figure 1B.

AFFINAL KINSHIP

Figures 1A and 1B clearly show descent lines. In contrast, let us look at another kind of relation. Clearly, your wife's sister is your sister-in-law, but what about her husband? Is he your brother-in-law, your WZH? Most of us probably will claim him unless he is particularly obnoxious, but if he is a brother-in-law, why not include his brothers? If you are puzzling over just how you are related to these people, note the following.

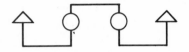

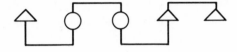

Figure 1C. A man's wife's
sister's husband.

Figure 1D. A man's wife's sister's
husband's brother.

Probably, few Americans would ever recognize WZHB as a relative unless a particular one was rich or famous.

Let us consider another type of relationship now, one that Americans never experience. In most parts of the world a man may marry several women, a practice called *polygyny*. Among the Nyoro of Africa, Beattie (1960:55–60) indicates that these women may be sisters (*sororal polygyny*). As co-wives they generally work well together. The wives each have a separate house but share a common household and farm the same fields. These co-wives are related to each other as husband's wife. A woman's child is related to her co-wife's children by marital links. The tie might better be described as MHWS, for example, rather than FWS. When trouble arises in the household, it seldom is a result of jealousy over a husband; rather, a woman fears her children are being deprived for the sake of a co-wife's children. Even though we are unfamiliar with co-wives, we can see immediately in this case familiar problems resulting from affinal relationships.

Regardless of the variety of "in-laws," what is the nature of this kin relation? Obviously, it is one created by marital ties. Anthropologists call it an *affinal tie*. Note that a consanguineal tie may be involved, as in wife's *sister*, but a marriage was essential as a basis for the relation. Intuitively, we feel some major differences between affinal and consanguineal ties.

Anthropology's first major study of kinship was entitled *Systems of Consanguinity and Affinity* (Morgan 1870). Can you think of any kinship ties that are not based on descent or marriage? Do you know any two specific people who are related but have no affinal or consanguineal link? All of you are likely to know of such a case.

PSEUDO-KINSHIP

In our society adopted children are recognized fully as relatives. The basis for the relationship is strictly a legal one; nevertheless, an adopted son is recognized the equal of a consanguineal son. In many other societies a ritual tie, rather than a legal one, is the basis for this type of kinship. In America, godparents are still known but probably few of you suggested them as real "relatives"; however, in Latin America the *padrinos* (godparents) are an important set of relatives. In Tepoztlán Lewis (1960:66) tells us that *padrinos* care for their godchildren in emergencies and adopt them if orphaned. Moreover, they have a close relation with the parents, addressing each other as *compadres*. *Compadres* have much respect for each other, but many mutual obligations bring them together like brothers and sisters. Relationships of this sort are known as *pseudo-kinship*. These ties are usually modeled after consanguineal ones. Pseudo-brotherhoods are created in many societies; generally the tie is much more like real brotherhood rather than what we experience in fraternities, unions, or other organizations called "brotherhoods."

KINSHIP BEHAVIOR

At this point it is well to consider further the nature of kinship. We have said the ties of kinship are based on consanguinity, affinity, or fictional links. When we talked about *who* a cousin is, we considered descent ties, but if we ask *what* a cousin is, we will have to talk about social relations. Obligations, duties, rights, and so forth define kin relations. First cousins are persons who cannot be married (at least in some states and in some religious denominations); ordinarily, we exchange gifts or cards with them; see them on special occasions; expect to help and be helped by them at times. However, a good friend often takes the place of a cousin among ourselves, depending on how far apart we live or possibly the good nature of cousin's spouse. In terms of in-law relations, it is more difficult to define what the relationship is between brothers-in-law. Americans allow much leeway in their behavior. Some of them see very little of each other and hardly consider themselves related. I was not altogether joking before when I said a WZHB might be very "close" if rich or famous—people will play up a kinship tie when it is to their advantage. They also may change the nature of the tie. Most in-law relations are potentially hostile, but a common cause between in-laws may well suppress the hostility. For instance, two men married to sisters (brothers-in-law) may have little in common until a domineering father-in-law appears; then they may well band together. Thus kinship behavior is a matter of context as well as personality.

If we examine a more intimate tie such as father and son, we still see leeway and manipulation in behavior. A father is obliged to provide food, shelter, help in education, and religious and political guidance. However, the rights and obligations of each to the other are an intricate mazeway with much variation even between the same individuals over time.

If you will compile a list of all the things a father "should do" for his son, the list will invariably detail economic, political, educational, health, or religious obligations. One is brought up sharply with the conclusion that there is no inherent content in the kin relation; that is, one cannot list behavior that is kinship behavior. One lists instead economic or religious behavior that is due a relative. This elementary point was only recently brought home to anthropologists who for a hundred years have been analyzing "kinship" in depth.

Still we are not convinced that kinship is only an aspect of other types of behavior. Too many novelists have delved into the father–son relationship in too great a depth to deny the uniqueness of the status relation. Obviously, affect and emotion are important qualities of kinship; unfortunately, it is much more difficult to document and describe these qualities of kinship or the uniqueness of emotions that attach to particular types of relations.

The quality of kin relations, therefore, is yet to be analyzed crossculturally. Instead, we have concentrated on how kin statuses are arranged in different communities, comparing these arrangements with residence patterns, ecological adjustments, and so forth. We have also been remiss in studying American kinship.

The initial studies are comparatively recent (Schneider and Homans 1955), and only one book-length treatment is available (Schneider 1968). The American system and the various other systems are described elsewhere (Schusky 1972); one example here will illustrate how statuses may be arranged differently.

THE STRUCTURES OF KIN TIES

The most common arrangement among peoples of the world is a system that equates your MZ with M and FB with F. There is only one word, that is, one status for however many relatives occupy this position *vis-à-vis* yourself. The MB is a distinct status from father and his brother. FZ is distinct from mother and mother's sister. Your brothers and sisters would be "the same" or "equated with" the children of your MZ and your FB. This system emphasizes that the children of MB and FZ are different (anthropologists designate them as *cross cousins*); indeed, they are often preferred as spouses. However, *parallel cousins*, children of MZ and FB, are so much like siblings that incest regulations completely block marriage with them.

An anthropologist's diagram for a system such as this one might look like the following, which documents the kinship terms used by a Dakota Indian for his close relatives. The Dakota speaker here is indicated as "Ego."

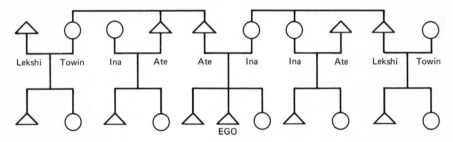

Figure 1E. Dakota terminology as supplied by Lower Brule Sioux Indians to author.

A kin arrangement of this type seems to knit small-scale communities together so that kinship can be the basis for almost all activity. It is such a common form of organization that anthropologists have coined a term for it, the *Iroquois System*. Actually, not all the Iroquois had such a form of kin grouping, but the Seneca did. These Iroquois were among the first people studied, and their form became the prototype for systems that equate parallel cousins with siblings while making cross cousins different. The classification is based solely on kinship terminology and not behavior. Unfortunately, behavior and terminology do not always coincide; the terms must be considered only a rough index to behavior, much as ideal behavior is related to real behavior.

The various ways by which relations are classified have long been a basic part of anthropology. Now we are looking more into the quality of kin relations and exploring more deeply the relationship between kinship and ecology. One classic study of the nineteenth century proposed that early man based all his relations on kinship but that during the course of social evolution territorial or national ties replaced kinship. Although this hypothesis can no longer be accepted, we still do not understand fully the relationship between territory and kinship. Yet it does seem certain that locale together with the way it is used is closely linked with kinship organization. Since all men have kinship as a basic part of their social organization, it is useful to examine the ways in which non-hominids without kinship relate to a locale—that is, primates who are well organized but lacking kinship might likely tell us something about the origin of kinship.

TIES OF NONHUMAN PRIMATES

To increase their knowledge about the ways in which kinship serves as a basic adaptation to habitat, anthropologists have been studying a variety of primates in the wild during the last decade. Behavior in the wild is often radically different from that observed in zoos. Usually studies must be carried out under difficult conditions for long periods of time, and the reports of such observations are still limited (DeVore 1965; Jay 1968). The initial researchers had to overcome the influence of Sigmund Freud and already existing studies of captive animals. Freud and artificial conditions had led anthropologists to assume that sex would be the all-important basis for social life.

Studies of free-ranging baboons quickly dispelled the importance of sex as a social force. Baboon troops in savanna or grasslands are built around a dominant male (as pictured by Freud), but this male is little concerned with exclusive rights to females. He does provide leadership for the troop and members pick up subtle clues from him about where to range and when to eat or retire. Most impressively, the dominant male joins with younger males against predators or other dangers that threaten the troop in what can only be described as complex cooperation: While the leader and three or four lieutenants ward off a cheetah or leopard, younger males hurry females and young to protective trees or cliffs. Nor is leadership always limited to one animal. A pair or trio may form a cooperating clique to give leadership. The leaders respond to sentries on the periphery who give initial alarms; the troop then responds as a whole. Communication for such complex response must be well developed. Observers have found that some baboons are capable of giving an "all clear" sound when an infant has cried out a "false alarm." Clearly, this baboon social organization rests on needs for defense in open grass country. In other locales with different ecological conditions baboon organization varies greatly from what is described here, but everywhere the social relationship is far more "political" than "sexual" (Tiger and Fox 1971).

Like human political organizations, baboon "politics" includes internal control and external defense of a territory. A baboon troop dwelling in savanna spends most of its time around a nesting area that offers night protection. Much of their feeding is close to this point and consists of a core area that is seldom "invaded" by other baboons, for intruders are attacked. Surrounding the core is a larger range where the troop sometimes feeds; this territory may overlap the range of another troop. When two troops meet in this area, a few animals intermingle although we suspect a smaller troop may occasionally join with a larger group to insure protection. What we did not expect was that baboon troops could be so stable and long-lasting. The average baboon probably spends his lifetime within the group where he was born and seldom leaves his home territory.

It is now also clear from the variety of organizations possible that these patterns of social life are learned in large part and that "instinctive" behavior is of little consequence. Therefore, baboons can adapt to a wide variety of habitats, adjusting their social forms to their environment. Thus some are found in fairly harsh, desertlike country, while others do well in lush savanna close to rain forest.

Of course, it is far more difficult to study primates living in dense rain forest or spending their lives in trees, but a few such studies are now complete. Generally, it appears that the more time a primate spends in open grassland, where predators abound, the more complex its social organization. However, gorillas are not preyed upon, except by man; yet they too have remarkably stable social lives. Again, sex has been found of little consequence for gorilla society, but it is not certain what binds gorillas to each other so tightly. Gorillas are also bound to a territory, a larger and not so clear-cut one as that of baboons. Although gorilla relations are on the whole more simple than those among baboons, gorillas are political; their groups have an organization for internal control and external relations.

Despite the wide variety of social forms among the nonhuman primates, we can conclude that much of social life is based on possession of territory. Locale is the foundation for social life, and social ties are wholly within the local group. What is learned in social life largely concerns defense or control of territory.

On the basis of these studies we can make some guesses about the life of early man. Imagine an upright primate, about chimpanzee size, who found himself spending his life in savanna country. How would he defend himself against predators? If he once became the hunter instead of the hunted, how would he accomplish the hunting? Cartoonists have oversimplified the solutions by picturing primitive man as simply picking up a club (as depicted in the movie *2001*). From what you know even now of primate social life, what do you think of such a simple answer? How do hunters and gatherers today differ from a baboon troop? We may never know when or exactly how the differences occurred, but the developments deriving from hunting are what make man a unique kind of social animal. Speculate on the difference before reading further.

THE KINSHIP TIES OF HOMINIDS

Certain distinctions can readily be made between the behavior of humans and nonhumans. First, in all human communities there is a strict division of labor. Among baboons both sexes forage equally, consuming independently of each other. Even the infant is taught quickly what he needs to know about eating and is soon independent. It is impossible to speak of any actual system of production, distribution, or consumption. Baboons are a "political" animal but never an economic one. Among humans a sexual division of labor is basic to organization and provides for a system of production, distribution, and consumption. Exactly what men or women do varies considerably—in a number of places men do the cooking; elsewhere they do the weaving—but sex-related tasks are always found. Thus human groups split in two to perform labor, and when they reunite the products of their work are distributed in ways that further unite the group. It is tempting to believe that the hunting adaptation caused the split. After all, man is the only primate who consistently hunts. Furthermore, among contemporary hunters a common pattern emerges, as men forage over a wide area, while women gather within a restricted range. When big game animals are hunted, this pattern is exaggerated. Teams of men must cooperate in tracking and killing over an extensive area. Men return to dole out meat in often complex ways, while women simply provide for themselves and their husbands.

In this process, men control most of the exchange, and it seems they go on to control politics as well. In all communities control is overtly in the hands of men. In some communities this power may be diminished because women assume considerable covert power, but everywhere men traditionally have been recognized as exercising overt control. This fact is a basic ingredient in human kinship.

Second, in the human community primary kin do not mate nor marry. The data on other primates is not clear, but it appears they tend to avoid such mating. The norms that prohibit such unions are called *incest rules.* Why such rules exist is not clear; in fact, it would seem to solve many of our problems if brothers and sisters did marry, as we will see later. In many communities close kin such as cross cousins do marry. Although you have been taught that close inbreeding is poor genetic practice, there is no evidence of it from cross-cousin marriage. A much more reasonable theory is that children reared in close proximity do not sexually appeal to each other as adults. But, if that is true why have a rule at all? Also, in many communities spouses have been reared in close proximity. The converse theory has it that mating and marrying outside the family establishes a wider network of relatives. These larger groupings are supposedly more "successful" somehow than the smaller intermarried group. If this theory is correct, one wonders why so many communities have *endogamous* norms, rules that require people to marry within a restricted range. These theories and others are evaluated at length by Aberle and others (1963).

One fact about incest is certain. It is uniquely human; no other primates have such a norm. And the fact that one cannot mate or marry primary kin means that one must marry beyond the primary kin. In short, incest prohibitions and marriage regulations are two sides of the same coin. The marriage regulations may be far more complex, but essentially they simply unite two or more units of primary kin. By such union, the elements of kinship are created. Incest prohibitions, in effect, define mother, father, sister, brother, son, and daughter. By this definition one must find a husband or wife outside this group. Thus we have ties of consanguinity and affinity.

In summary, the human group, like other primates, occupies a territory and comprises a complex society. Humans form a unique kind of group, however, because kinship ties are basic to their social life. Within the group, kinship governs most behavior; more importantly, kin ties link any one local group with many others. The ways these links are established vary among communities. The crosscultural comparison of the various ways has provided some of our most thorough understanding of human behavior, and such comparisons are the subject of Chapters 3 and 4. In the next chapter we will examine simply the logical possibilities of group formations, given the "facts of life": Men control most of the power, and incest requires people to marry out of the immediate family.

EXERCISE

1. Professional genealogists are interested only in lineal ancestors; their branching diagrams reflect this interest. They usually proceed from Ego, John Jones in this case, in the following manner:

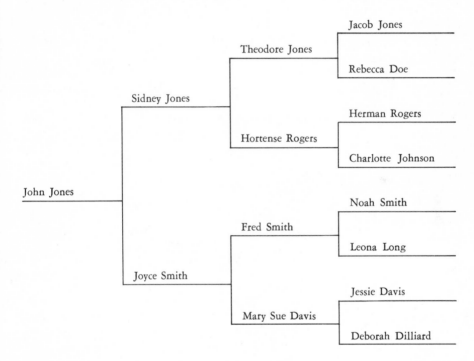

Anthropologists and others interested in kin behavior realize that collateral relatives, the uncles and aunts and cousins, are more significant in everyday life. Draw a diagram of the type used by anthropologists that includes all of your relatives to whom you recognize any tie. A deceased relative may be noted with an X through his symbol, a divorce is noted by an X through the tie, that is, the horizontal line between spouses. If your diagrams are compared in class, you are likely to find some that include only three or four generations, others with eight or more.

Low birth rates during the depression are often reflected in numbers of siblings in the appropriate generation. Ethnic or rural students often have to use a second or third sheet to include all their relatives, while many other students do not fill a single sheet. Comparison of the genealogies is most useful to emphasize the point of the range of variations in American kinship.

SUGGESTED READINGS FROM THE CASE STUDIES SERIES*

John Beattie, *Bunyoro: An African Kingdom.* Chapter 5 describes kin relations in a specific setting. Some of the details may be perplexing for the student at this point, but the chapter brings out important differences between consanguineal and affinal relations unfamiliar to Westerners. The Bunyoro case will be reviewed further in a later chapter as well.

Oscar Lewis, *Tepoztlán: Village in Mexico.* Pages 66–69 introduce the subject of ritual kinship. Since the topic is not covered elsewhere in this unit, the case study is a useful reference; furthermore, this particular ritual relation is important because it is so widely spread through Latin America.

OTHER READINGS

Lionel Tiger and Robin Fox, *The Imperial Animal.* Chapter 1 summarizes the variation in social life among the nonhuman primates, indicating how a primate past must influence human behavior. Chapter 2 spells out the relation between a primate biogrammer, or innate program, and political organization.

* For complete information on listed titles see Bibliography at end of book.

2

Types of Kin Groups

The locus of control in males and the universal presence of incest rules force problems on human territorial groups that no other primates have. As culture developed, groups came into possession of things, including certain rights to land, tools, clothing, and other artifacts. Property and rights had to be passed on, just as culture is transmitted, to younger generations. The simplest way for this inheritance to take place would have been for brothers and sisters to marry. Fathers would then pass on their property and status prerogatives to their sons; daughters would inherit from their mothers. Siblings who had learned from birth how to get along with each other should do well as husband and wife. But incest rules prohibit such a rational approach to family life.

Given incest regulations and male authority within any group, what possibilities exist for family formations? What logical groups can you hypothesize? Could a group of sisters send off their brothers to mate with other women while they themselves took a series of lovers, thus composing a group of sisters with their children? Early travelers often described such a group, usually somewhere near the Amazon. But could an Amazon society exist? No, because male control would be absent, and it has been described as a prerequisite of family groups (Fox 1967).

However, such a situation has been approximated. Among the Nayar of South India the young woman would take a husband whom she would seldom see. A series of lovers then visited her, and children were conceived mostly by these men. Neither the husband nor the lovers formed any close attachment to the wife or their women and children. Traditionally, Nayar men were warriors. It is possible that the acquisition of necessary skills demanded so much time that they could not afford the usual ties of husband and fatherhood. Still, the Nayar man assumed important control in one household—that of his mother. The man had significant ritual and political tasks in his mother's household, and corresponding rights and responsibilities toward his sisters and sisters' children. In sum, the core of any household was a group of sisters and their children; although brothers were frequently absent and never fathered any of the children, they remained in the household to exercise traditional male authority.

The Nayar are well known because of one oddity—that they approach having a household without males or a family without marriage. However, Gough (1962) has shown that the Nayar were not exceptional, for they follow the practices of male control and incest regulation. Moreover, some of their "oddities" are a result of being a group within groups. They desired their women to marry into a higher

11

strata even if the "husband" had virtually no responsibility for his "wife." Thus marriage practices were dependent upon Nayar relations within a larger society and make much greater sense in this context. Possibly, further confusion exists over Nayar "exceptions" or "oddities" because knowledge of their practices is largely historical reconstruction based on rather vague data. However, for our purposes the Nayar illustrate how closely a family can come toward dispensing with husbands and reducing male controls. But recall that the Nayar are noted for unusual family organization. What is a more likely pattern, one that is close to the Nayar form? You probably have guessed it because you have heard of matriarchal peoples.

Before describing this pattern, let us discard the idea of matriarchy. If our claim is correct that men universally exercise the power, then matriarchy is a misleading concept. It arose from situations something like the following. Upon marriage a man would go to live with his wife, who would be in a household with her sisters. The house and property would belong to the group of women, these women and their children forming a line or lineage. A husband would remain a member of his mother's lineage. A man's children would belong to his wife's lineage, and since men would marry out of their lineage (a practice called *exogamy*), children would always belong to a lineage different from their fathers. A man in this situation is in the uncomfortable position of finding his wife allied with a host of consanguineal relatives, and in time of difficulty he may be forced out of his home. In some societies a wife simply places her husband's few personal belongings outside the door; when he discovers these, he knows he is divorced. The shock is alleviated, of course, because a man can always go home to his mother. Indeed, the trouble with the wife quite possibly arose because the man had been spending too much time in his mother's household in the first place, for that is where he has political, ritual, and some economic control. He is also needed there to oversee his sisters' sons, who are in his lineage. You can appreciate why a Western observer might describe such a society as matriarchal. Women seem to have much control, yet it is invariably men who exercise overt power, although it is within the sisters' households rather than the wife's. Even in the wife's home, the man may beat and berate her and will usually not do the menial work of women, even in this kind of society.

The situation can be pictured by a diagram. The shaded symbols in Figure 2A are those persons who comprise the lineage. The outlined section includes those who form a residence group.

HURON, MATRILINEAL AND MATRILOCAL

The above model is a logical possibility and allows us to anticipate what may in fact occur, although any particular ethnographic case will differ from it in some detail. The Huron Indians of eastern North America serve as a good example. Like the Nayar, the Huron changed sufficiently so that some ethnographic detail may be invalid. Trigger (1969:54–68) has reconstructed Huron society insofar as possible and pictures a society somewhat like the one just described.

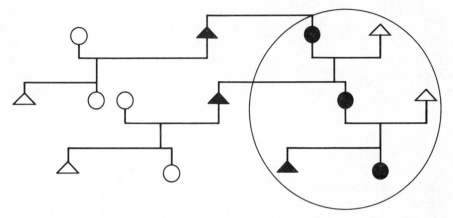

Figure 2A. Differences between lineage membership and residence group.

The Huron occupied New York and southern Ontario when first contacted by the French. Soon they were important figures in the fur trade, and the new economy altered their old ways. Still they continued to follow a pattern in which men joined their wives after marriage in matrilocal residence. A wife lived with her mother and sisters, and probably her mother's sister and her children, in a longhouse. Each family unit had its own fireplace, but the longhouse was essentially a single household.

The women and their children in a household constituted a lineage, but the Huron were little interested in genealogies so lineages had little depth. However, each Huron lineage claimed membership in a larger grouping called a *clan*. The clans were groups with such names as Bear, Beaver, and Turtle. The Huron assumed that any member of Turtle lineage had a common ancestory with all other Turtles. With such ancestory the consanguineal tie was so close that two members of the same clan could not marry.

In addition to exogamy, clans controlled political office. Each lineage, or *clan segment* as Trigger describes them, had its own chiefs, responsible for internal affairs and representative to larger units such as the village, tribe, or confederacy. The segment was the primary unit for protecting an individual, seeking vengeance for him, or securing reparations. Men gained office and secured prestige through their lineage. Of course, succession to such office was through a mother's brothers rather than one's father.

The description so far closely follows the logical model, but some important discrepancies occurred in the usual Huron pattern. Commonly, male activities such as hunting and, later, fur trapping tended to keep men away from their villages and in scattered groups, particularly at certain times of the year. Frequent warfare contributed to a male mortality rate higher than that for women, who remained at the longhouse, working gardens and caring for children. Such factors would seem to encourage matrilocal households or at least make them the most stable form of extended family.

Many of the French accounts, however, describe households where wives were living with husbands in patrilocal residence. Such a situation allows a man to live where he holds office. And would not the French most likely be in contact with officeholders? That is, the French accounts were probably biased by the nature of their contact. They dealt with the higher leaders, whose duties may well have made them deviate from the common matrilocal residence.

Many peoples have had to face the Huron dilemma of how to form households around women and yet dwell where the men will hold office. Some of them have solved the problem by a device known as *avunculocal residence*. Trigger suspects at least a few Huron discovered the solution, but he admits he lacks positive evidence for it. In avunculocal residence, a young man went to live with his mother's brother. He found a wife in or near the household of his mother's brother so he enjoyed the advantages of matrilocal residence, while also being near the man he would succeed. If the practice is followed consistently, it leads to households composed of a man and his nephews rather than a woman and her daughters. However, the practice might well have been limited to the lineages of chiefs or the families that the Jesuits and other French would have known best.

Finally, Trigger notes that the Huron may not have had any strict rules of residence. A couple may have chosen a longhouse simply on the basis of space available or personal preference. It is almost certain that such factors did determine the choice of some people. Ward Goodenough (1951) has documented the problem by a detailed study of residence on the small Pacific island of Truk. Many exceptions to the rule of matrilocal residence occurred. It seems likely that, just as on Truk, most married couples did reside most of the time with the wife's lineage, for matrilocal residence was the norm. It was expected of a Huron couple, but just as we expect a newly married couple to establish a new household, we know of many who do not. There is the young man who must move in with his mother-in-law because his bride must care for her; there is the son-in-law who must move in with his bride because her father's mansion is so large it can house another family. In short, just as personal considerations bring deviation from the American norm of neolocality, some Huron deviated for similar reasons.

The Huron case illustrates a pattern, fairly common in the world, where women and their daughters form a core group. Membership in the group is inherited only through females, and inheritance is matrilineal. Males of the group become loosely attached to the lineages of their wives, but only as household members. Throughout life the males remain members of their mother's lineage, and they return there for political and ritual rights and responsibilities. Their residence is termed matrilocal, but residence rules must be understood generally to permit much leeway.

As anthropologists studied such matters they came slowly to understand residence practices, in the meantime applying "matrilocal" to what were in fact quite different practices. Think what is likely to happen under conditions slightly different from those the Huron faced. A variety of clans existed in every Huron village, and a man could marry outside his lineage and clan while remaining in or near his childhood home. If a village were composed only or mostly of one matrilineage, then men of the lineage would have to find brides much farther away. Thus lineage duties for men in such a situation became much more onerous.

AVUNCULOCAL RESIDENCE

One solution, of course, is avunculocal residence, which in some cases is indistinguishable from matrilocal residence. A man goes to live with his mother's brother, who will pass on lineage knowledge, rights, and obligations. The mother's brother will also be interested in finding a wife for his sister's son; indeed, his own daughter is a possible spouse. She belongs to a different lineage yet her father has some influence over her marriage. The practice of regularly marrying the mother's brother's daughter is uncommon, but it has been found in a diverse number of places. It is termed *matrilateral cross-cousin marriage*. The practice is diagrammed below.

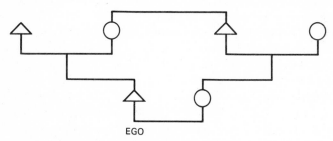

EGO

Figure 2B. Matrilateral cross-cousin marriage.

Given matrilineal descent, local exogamy, and widely spaced villages, however, what seems more likely to occur? Where are men likely to exert their authority?

Obviously the men must either compromise the matrilocal rule or gain influence in their wife's lineage (this latter an alternative to be examined in depth in Chapter 4). The first solution, compromise of residence, is well illustrated by the Micronesian atoll of Ulithi (pronounced *You*-li-thee).

ULITHI, MATRILINEAL AND PATRILOCAL

William Lessa (1966) tells us early in *Ulithi: A Micronesian Design for Living* that the major source of conflict among these islanders is land. Land disputes arise because ownership is along matrilineal lines, while actual tenure follows patrilineal principles. This apparent contradiction serves as a warning that one must take careful note of all that is involved in land ownership and use. Let us look at some ethnographic detail to see why the Ulithi have combined patrilocal residence with matrilineal descent.

Coconuts are a major food source in Ulithi life. The nut is eaten raw or cooked in all stages of growth; its milk is regularly drunk, and a kind of toddy is made from the tree sap. The leaves are used for roof thatches, baskets, mats, and, of course, girls' skirts. The trunk is essential for house beams, and even the root is a medicinal ingredient. The care of trees—the toddy harvest is especially arduous—is considered men's work.

Root crops such as taro and sweet potato also contribute much to Ulithi diet, with some breadfruit, bananas, and sugarcane also available. These crops require fairly constant attention, and although women do much of this cultivating, men perform much of the more strenuous tasks and are not above weeding and harvesting. Men also do much of the cooking.

The diet is rounded out by fishing, and many varieties are caught mostly by net. The most successful expeditions involve fairly large numbers of men operating out of canoes, as they fish the lagoon at length. Men have rights to traditional fishing grounds, and women supplement harvest of the lagoon by the gathering of littoral shellfish.

To best utilize the atoll's resources the people had to scatter over the islands in fairly small villages, for, with only one exception, each island could support only one village. Few villages, if any, ever exceeded a population of 100. While villages are built compactly on the lagoon shore, root crops are grown in more distant swamps, with bananas and coconuts usually close by. Dominating each village is a men's house, where activities center and political decisions are made. A canoe shed lines the beach and burial grounds flank the village.

There is reason to believe that Ulithians were formerly matrilocal like other neighboring Micronesians, but today they may be more accurately described as being patrilocal. Since their villages are small, inhabitants most often look to other islands for mates. Initially, a man may live with his wife's kin to perform bride service. He recognizes that her removal from her family will cause economic loss, and he compensates his in-laws by working for them a year or two. After the couple returns to the groom's village, the wife becomes an integral part of the community. She may find other lineage mates in the village, or she may return with her husband to her native village for long stretches of time. The lure of her village is strong because she usually retains rights to land there.

From such village composition one must expect considerable flexibility in social forms. Three major forms of organization described by Lessa do, indeed, show wide variation, for great latitude seems a necessary ingredient in Ulithi life. The first form of organization, the nuclear family, composed of parents and children, is a good example. In a sample of households only one-fourth were actually comprised of nuclear families. Various kinds of kinsmen were generally attached to the nucleus, and frequent adoption and remarriage further complicated nuclear family life. The result of such practices is that feeding, sheltering, training, and other services commonly provided by the American nuclear family are so dissipated among the Ulithi that the nuclear family is comparatively less important, although sexual, reproductive, and some economic functions do center on the Ulithi nuclear family.

The second form of organization described by Lessa provides some of the services usually ascribed to the nuclear family; these are taken over in Ulithi by what Lessa terms the *commensal group*. Although commensal groups revolve around nuclear families, they are usually larger, with individual choice determining membership. Thus nuclear family members often share in different commensal groups, these groups not always formed on the basis of households, for an individual may eat in a group without any of the members with whom he lives. Eating in Ulithi is not regularly scheduled, but generally a large evening meal brings commensal members together. In such daily contact, plans may be made for economic activity such as fishing, where some group cooperation is necessary. Thus the commensal group replaces the extended family or other kin group that might serve similar purposes in other communities. Although membership in the commensal group is shifting because of its voluntary nature, most groups are fairly stable.

The third significant group in Ulithi society is the *lineage*, whose functions relate largely to land. Most land is regarded as the common property of particular lineages. Matrilineal descent affiliates the child with his maternal kinsfolk for certain social purposes, and identification with the lineage is based on a common name and ancestor. Leaders within a lineage assign members rights to work certain sections, but individual ownership of a tract is inconceivable. Lineage activity revolves around twenty active lines, but twenty other defunct ones are maintained through custodianship. The lineages of some recent immigrants are also recognized.

Any individual, of course, can only be a member of one lineage. Most Ulithi are always members of their mother's lineage, although in adoption a switchover may occur. Much more importantly, an individual has ties to numerous other lineages. A man may gain from his wife's lineage and father's lineage as well as his own. He will also be in significant contact with other lineages represented in his commensal group and to a lesser extent within his village. By one means or another, an individual is able to establish some relationship with all the other lineages. Ordinarily it is of little advantage to do so, but if the occasion arises, the possibility exists.

Now let us return to the earlier question of why the Ulithi combine patrilocality with matrilineal descent. Logically such a combination makes little sense, and you should see clearly that part of the problem is a semantic one. The Ulithi are not really patrilocal, for their residence rules are quite flexible and allow them to take advantage of any available land. Likewise, commensal groups provide further flexibility through voluntary, sometimes shifting membership. Not only can an individual change residence, he can also change eating partners within the residence area. Lineage membership, on the other hand, is fixed; however, individuals are capable of utilizing links to most other lineages. Father's and wife's lineages are especially close, but links can be established on a non-kin basis as well.

It is tempting to tie this exceptional flexibility of Ulithi social organization to the ecology of a Pacific atoll. The small islands are capable of supporting only a small population, and the norms must allow individuals to move readily to take advantage of unused land. However, it is very difficult to prove such a hypothesis. For the present at least, you should simply keep in mind that one form of human grouping consists of a membership group formed by descent through females but more or less scattered with their husbands, who locate on the basis of multiple purposes.

Let us return to other possibilities of group formations. The Ulithi suggest an obvious one based on their patrilocal residence. If men regularly live with their fathers, then brothers stay together, possessing property and status, which they pass on to their sons. Membership within such a group, determined by descent through males, is called *patriliny* or *patrilineal descent*. A man succeeds his father rather than his mother's brother; in turn his son, instead of sister's son, will inherit from him.

With patrilineal descent authority is always kept within the lineage. In-marrying females cannot ever gain power in patrilineal groups the way in-marrying males sometimes acquire it in matrilineal societies. Residence can vary and even be matrilocal, but patrilocality is to be expected. Compared to matriliny, there is not much variation from a model of patriliny. Patrilineal, patrilocal peoples consist of a line of men who live close together in solidarity and bring in outside wives whose brothers have little influence in their sisters' lineage. Frequently, a bride price or bride wealth accompanies patriliny. It functions to remove a child from any claims of its mother's lineage; thus progeny price might be a better term than bride price. In short, the practice illustrates how tightly bound the patrilineage becomes.

Patrilineality is much more widespread than matrilineality and became well known to anthropology early in its history. A stereotypic picture of patrilineality grew up, and in fairness it should be reiterated that patrilineal societies do have many similarities. So it was some time before anthropologists realized just how variable patrilineal societies can be.

IGBO, PATRILINEAL AND PATRILOCAL

Chapter 4 allows a thorough examination of patrilineal principles in comparison with matrilineal ones, but, for the present, we will just look briefly at two patrilineal communities to see the extent of variation possible under the one scheme of forming groups through males. The Igbo of West Africa afford some sharp contrasts with the Gururumba of New Guinea. Since much of our understanding of patriliny, and even social organization, grew out of early work in West Africa, it should come as no surprise that the Igbo well fit the patrilineal prototype. Uchendu (1965) provides us with an insider's view of this tribe in *The Igbo of Southeast Nigeria*. Their community straddles the Niger River just above its delta, and although the people are divided into two political units, they remained one in culture and identity.

Igbo subsistence is based upon yam, manioc, and taro. These roots provide a large yield but require cheap labor and abundant land. The value of land is recognized in many ways and has acquired emotional meanings. Although people strive to acquire more land, individual ownership of land is prohibited. Land ownership is limited to the lineage, and individual members have security of tenure for home and farm lands; no member goes without land. Ideally, a lineage cannot dispose of land (thus it could not acquire land either), but the Igbo have actually institutionalized ways of alienating land. We may conclude that (1) competition for land is keen, and (2) lineages rather than individuals compete.

Much of the zest of life, therefore, is bound up in lineage organization, and the whole society can be mapped into a number of *agnatic* (another word for patrilineal) groups. Uchendu tells us (1965:64) that *agnation* determines membership of a family group, the line of inheritance and succession to name and office, and a person's final rights to land. An Igbo proverb expresses it: "Agnates are the source of one's strength." The lineage supports a man's claims against other lineages; it is where a man brings his wife and rears his children. Title-taking ceremonies, marriage feasts, and second-burial rites all succeed or fail, depending upon interpersonal relations among a person and his agnates. Even in death an Igbo prays to be buried in the lineage's ancestral land; ordinarily a woman must be returned to her homeland for burial among kinsmen.

Obviously agnates are the major source of support, but they also drive one to success, because the lineage is judged by all its members. Igbo lineages were particularly forceful; under the British they forced members to succeed at education. "Progress" became a major value, and Igbo success eventually led them to secede from Nigeria to become the state of Biafra. Obviously then agnates must be a source of hostility as well as support. Uchendu reports the Igbo describe this ambivalence by saying an agnate is the most likely to help but also the most likely to kill. Or, as a proverb has it, "The house rat, not the bush rat, knows where the condiments are."

The intralineage striving mixes much competition with cooperation, and the process causes hostility. It is one's agnates who accuse and convict one of sorcery. Wives manifest aggression through gossip, ridicule, and slander. It is directed at co-wives or husband's brothers' wives. Although the wives are not of the lineage, it is obvious how much aggression they will stir up within the compound and lineage. Soon a man is challenging a lineage brother to a wrestling contest or carrying the matter to the lineage head.

So much of life is wrapped up in lineage organization that a man becomes involved with, if not a member in, other lineages. For the Igbo, the mother's lineage is of next importance after his own. His relationship to it is in marked contrast with his own. In it he is an honorary member where he is made most welcome. Since he is not a competitor with mother's agnates, they are ready to comfort him and more importantly to protect or arbitrate his jural rights in his own patrilineage. In times of trouble mother's lineage is also a refuge for the convicted sorcerer, and in times of celebration it can be counted on for gifts and feasting.

The tie to mother's lineage is permanent, and her death only strengthens the bond because sons are expected to bury the mother as well as father. Funerals are expensive, and the son must contribute heavily to aid mother's lineage, which is ultimately responsible for its members, even in death. Mother's brothers remain after her death, and a man has very special ties to them.

Uchendu's description of the mother's brother–sister's son relationship is a vivid one because as an Igbo he is personally familiar with it. Since he catches the underlying spirit in it that most other anthropologists have missed, his description (1965: 66–67) deserves full attention. He reports that the mother's brother's advice always succeeds when that of others has failed. His great influence stems from friendship and love rather than the fear-inducing superiority that the father maintains. In Igbo thought, mother's brother and sister's son are so close because they were held by the same navel cord, a fact which allows many privileges. A number of taboos marks the sister's son as a special guest when he is at his mother's brother's home. He cannot be physically abused—it would seriously offend the Earth

Goddess if he were to bleed—and he is expected to take advantage of the situation. He jokes at the expense of mother's father as well as her brother and especially at their wives. He may take anything he wants without permission, and Igbo regularly exploit the fruit trees and liquor supply of their mother's brothers. Obviously, a man is closely tied to his mother's brother's lineage so much so that the tie carries over to his children. Thus an Igbo is bound to his mother's mother's lineage, although these kin are recognized as more "remote" than mother's own lineage. Likewise, father's mother's agnates are recognized as remote kinsmen, but still close enough that marriage is prohibited with all such relatives.

Thus an Igbo recognizes important ties to four lineages. He can travel over a wide area and feel at home in a distant village if he finds kinsmen in one of these lineages. Most of us are immediately curious about the relationship a man creates upon marriage. What does the lineage of a wife mean to a man? Before looking at the ethnographic detail, you should try to answer this question for yourself. Will the wife's lineage be a source of affect and comfort, or will a man encounter hostility among his in-laws?

Uchendu's method for describing the relationship is most revealing. While we think of it as wife's lineage, he denotes it as "son's mother's lineage." A man pays progeny price to another lineage, one not linked to him through his mother, mother's mother, or father's mother. This payment is the source of continual friction, and betrothing may take years and involve middlemen. Furthermore, it is a contract between lineages rather than individuals, and, as many people became involved in the marriage, the possibilities of misunderstanding multiply. Several stages, such as testing the girl's character, precede the bride price or progeny price. All these steps may cause difficulties, but progeny price almost guarantees trouble. Uchendu seems to take pride in the skill with which his people haggle, and settling a progeny price is an ideal occasion to demonstrate their abilities. Middlemen and representatives of both lineages explore good and bad features of a prospective bride; claims of generosity and miserliness revolve around the groom's lineage. Even after agreement, the payment is stretched out over years, and different "interpretations" and "memories" serve to agitate relations between the respective lineages as well as families.

These kinds of relationships have long been familiar to anthropology as functional parts of patriliny, and when people in another part of the world were described as patrilineal, it was assumed that they more or less fit the model as well as the Igbo do. The common pattern was of a rigidly patrilocal people, whose economic, political, and religious life occurred within the lineage. Ancestors were venerated in ritual. Mother's lineage and especially mother's brother were a source of affect and comfort, while wife's lineage was in a hostile relationship. Since some hostility was present within one's own lineage, feelings were usually ambivalent. These features were accepted as characterizing patrilineages generally.

More recent work, however, suggests that other peoples fit this model less rather than more. The patrilineal principle of forming lineages on the basis of descent through males can occur with fairly wide variation in other features. This discovery arose largely out of work in Melanesia, and the Gururumba well illustrate one form of the variation.

GURURUMBA, PATRILINEAL WITH VARIABLE RESIDENCE

Philip Newman (1965) reports in *Knowing the Gururumba* that membership of a significant group of the Gururumba is created through male links. Ascent to a common ancestor cannot be precisely traced but is implicit, and feelings that the relation is close are expressed by an exogamous rule. People have standing within this group, and succession occurs only through male links. Succession is of such importance that kinship terminology parallels it; a man calls his father and the leader of the group by the same term; elder brothers and others ahead of a man in the line of succession are called *uBono*; younger brothers and other heirs of a man are equated as *nakunE*. (Later chapters will more fully detail the correlation between kin groups and kinship terminology.) The Gururumba have no word to designate this significant membership group, but they describe it as "those who sit together," a phrase emphasizing the solidarity of this group. Solidarity and identification of members with the group also are expressed through vengeance rules; a murder obligates group members to take revenge, and vengeance is satisfied by the death of anyone in the murderer's lineage. Finally, this group performs certain festivals with religious overtones.

Few anthropologists would quarrel with Newman when he labels this group a *sib*, his word for a union of several lineages. This organization is much like the Igbo, in whose tribe the patrilineages were grouped in a larger organization that Uchendu called a *clan*. Whereas Igbo clans (or sibs) were outweighed in importance by the patrilineage, Gururumba patrilineages are subordinate to sibs. (Sib and clan are usually synonyms, but some anthropologists define sib as several lineages, clan as a residential group.)

Such a difference is comparatively minor, but Newman reports other features of Gururumba clans that do differentiate them from the Igbo patrilineal descent groups. Less focus on the group is indicated by lack of name or totem for either the lineage or clan. Actual descent ties are poorly remembered and membership is largely imputed; kin ties are implicit or taken on faith. The putative nature of group membership contrasts sharply with the Igbo's strict adherence to descent as the only means to membership. The leeway allowed by Gururumba permits some significant differences to develop. First, village settlement does not follow descent lines. Parts of as many as fifteen lineages would occupy a village; thus villagers use personal names among themselves rather than kinship terms. Because choice is possible, some women remain in their natal villages, where they may have land rights, an obverse of the Ulithi practice. About one-quarter of Gururumba households are matrilocal, and the women in these homes are apt to voice their opinion among their agnates in clan affairs, a practice other women cannot follow. In a case like this, mother's brother's lineage is likely to assert authority over a man because of their village leadership. Therefore, regularly structured relations toward mother's brother involving affect and support cannot develop as they do with Igbo. Nor is it feasible to maintain essentially hostile relations with wife's descent group if one is living in its vlllage.

Of course, it is inaccurate to speak of "its" village since a village is not limited to one descent group, but some descent groups do figure more importantly than others. Newman (1965:36) describes the major descent group of a village as "a unit recruiting some of its members on the basis of patrilineal descent . . . and on the basis of several other criteria as well."

These other criteria are much more difficult to define. They are a part of what goes into being a "Big Man." Big Men are political leaders who win their place by oratory, bluff, wealth, bravery, skill in war, and a host of other characteristics. If a man has many agnates in a village, it is more likely that he will become a Big Man than if he were without kin. Kin ties, however, do not guarantee succession to leadership; sons of Big Men often become Big Men, but they must earn the title— they do not inherit it.

You can see that the Gururumba allow much more leeway than Igbo in choice of leaders and village membership. It is possible that an emphasis upon warfare in New Guinea required more flexibility in social organization than in Africa. The causes, however, are far from clear, but it is obvious that the village in New Guinea, for whatever reasons, assumed many of the functions of Igbo clans.

Recount for yourself how a Gururumba village is like an Igbo clan. Newman (1965:36) presents an extensive list of village to clan similarities.

Most students find that matrilineal and patrilineal descent make a good deal of sense; indeed, a few will impute patrilineal descent for themselves simply on the basis of inheritance of surname. But your kinship group is considerably different from Huron or Igbo; those peoples eliminated one sex or the other as a basis for establishing a kin membership group. Americans really have nothing like a unilineal descent group. What do we have instead? Most of us have only parents, siblings, aunts, uncles, and cousins, a group that lasts only for a generation. Similar groups, of course, take its place, but the particular group you belong to is good only for your lifetime. Some of you may feel cheated at this because you intuitively realize that other "families" do last more than one generation. The Roosevelts, Rockefellers, and Du Ponts do not disappear quite like the Smiths and Jones. To comprehend such subtle differences it will be better to look at a seemingly quite exotic people. In this case the Kalinga of the Philippines can serve as a "mirror" for us to see ourselves.

KALINGA, COGNATIC DESCENT GROUPS

Edward Dozier (1967) pictures for us in *The Kalinga of Northern Luzon, Philippines* a mountain people scattered over a fairly large region with some differences developing between the branches in the north and south. Generally, the north is less densely settled and people depend on dry rice farming; in the south wet rice farming brings a denser population. In both areas the nuclear family is important, and husband, wife, and children, occasionally with an elderly parent, occupy a house. Close relatives, usually the wife's, are nearby, and two or three households comprise an extended family. Affect and emotional support are important functions of the nuclear family, while the extended family acts as an economic unit. Matrilocal residence is an ideal, but if parents have many daughters, it is likely that one or more will settle with the groom's family. Influential or wealthy parents are also likely to keep their sons and daughters-in-law with them. Further, the Kalinga are ready to take advantage of a new opportunity and often will reside neolocally to work better fields. Thus real behavior differs considerably from the norm of matrilocality.

Under such conditions ties with kin resemble those of your own. An American son may inherit a business or position from his father; on the other hand, he may marry the boss's daughter. He is even more likely to start his own business. Given such conditions one is tied more or less equally to relatives of both sexes or as you think of it: to both mother and father. Relations are extended upward through them to grandparents and to the sides (the technical term for this relation is *collateral*) to aunts and uncles. The point is that relations are two-sided or *bilateral*. The relationships depend upon you (or any particular person); only you and your siblings share exactly the same relatives. Dozier designates this group as the personal kindred; let us shorten it to *kindred*. All peoples have kindreds, but for Huron or Igbo the lineages far overshadow them. Among the Kalinga lineages are absent, and the kindred is all important, at least parts of the kindred. For instance, a typical Kalinga youth grows up in a house in intimate contact with siblings and parents. Daily he is also in contact with his mother's father and mother, his mother's sisters and their children, and possibly mother's brothers. Kalinga move over considerable distances and in the process maintain fairly close contact with father's relatives—his parents, his brothers, and their children. All these relatives have some responsibility for providing a man with a house and helping him in time of trouble. They further stand ready to help economically, either lending money or making land available.

All this behavior is characteristic of the northern Kalinga, who are most like you and me. Descent is bilateral, a person is tied equally to relatives on both sides, but permanent descent groups do not form. Among southern Kalinga, however, a variation on this pattern occurs. Dozier tells us of three exceptional instances in which families owned extensive irrigated rice fields; here behavior resembled that of many other groups in the Mountain Province of Luzon. Prominent ancestors are regarded as "founding fathers," and many people claim ascent to them. The links can be *through either sex*. A mountain tribesman may speak with pride of his mother's father's mother's father, ignoring other grandparents, just as many American women establish their rights to D.A.R. membership. Dozier describes the resulting structure of a *bilateral descent group* (it is also called a *cognatic descent group*) as a pyramid. The base is composed of the many people who trace their common tie through several paths to one prominent ancestor. A southern Kalinga may be motivated by pride in establishing such a link, but he probably is more interested in establishing land or water rights that have become associated with what is in effect a descent group. Remember it is a cognatic descent group rather than a unilineal descent group. Now, what parallels do you see between this Kalingan and a descendant of a founder of the Du Pont Corporation? Would you expect stratification or social classes in association with *cognatic descent groups*? What kind of stratification, if any, occurs among Kalinga?

Stratification alone does not necessarily cause cognatic descent groups. Dozier argues that for the Mountain Province they occur with a well-established wet rice complex, rigidity of ownership and inheritance of land, high population density, and clearly defined rules of water rights. When some families are able to gain economic advantage from these factors, they then form descent groups. The process is not entirely conscious; it is simply the result of men making claims to production on the basis of descent, a descent that may be traced through either sex.

Among many of the Kalinga, particularly in the north, dry rice is grown, water and land rights are not so important, and men shift residence easily. A man is little concerned in establishing ties to a remote ancestor in order to gain membership in a descent group. Indeed, there are no descent groups; a man's life is wrapped up simply in his nuclear and extended families with further ties to his kindred. The situation is a very familiar one to us, one in which we are most comfortable. Like the Kalinga most of us are not tied by kinship to any corporate group controlling property; we are highly mobile and can make use of kinship ties in our movement, but we do not allow them to bind us to a locale.

SUMMARY

In summary, the five case studies used as examples in this chapter supply a good introduction to how men universally have formed groups within a territory while observing incest regulations and overt male control. The major contrast is between unilineal descent and bilateral descent. The Huron and Ulithi indicate that considerable variation may occur among peoples in which descent is through females. The Igbo and Gururumba show us that variation among patrilineal peoples is also possible but need not be so great. Whether descent is through males or females, the resulting descent groups show a number of common characteristics that will be detailed in Chapter 4, which also explores further the differences between matriliny and patriliny.

Unilineal descent once seemed much different from bilateral descent because we thought descent groups would not be feasible given the large number of ties possible if both sexes figure in descent. For a long time, then, after anthropologists had discovered bilateral descent groups, they tried to argue that the groups were either patrilineal or matrilineal. The discovery of the cognatic descent group led us to realize that considerable option is possible in a descent group, and this realization forced reevaluation of unilineal descent groups. In the more recent examination we have discovered in the unilineal system greater flexibility than we had previously assumed. Of course, the greater flexibility means a wider variation.

Further and more intensive examination of the different kinships systems is, therefore, necessary. The next chapter offers a variety of cases in which bilateral descent results, on the one hand, simply in the nuclear family and kindred, and, on the other hand, in bilateral descent groups. Cases in Chapter 4 illustrate common characteristics for all unilineal descent groups and inherent differences between matrilineages and patrilineages. Chapter 5 introduces the subject of the ways in which marriage allies descent groups and the different functions it assumes in communities where descent groups are absent.

EXERCISES

1. Review in Figure 2A the way matriliny and matrilocality are diagrammed. Construct your own diagram showing patriliny and patrilocality.

2. Read pages 65–74 of Frederick Gamst, *The Qemant*, in the Case Studies Series to see how this people conforms to the model illustrated by your diagram. Descent groups will follow the line of descent in the model. Can you show in the diagram how the Qemant determine land rights and customs of mutual aid? This inheritance is along "ambilineal" lines, following the same principle as cognatic descent groups.

SUGGESTED READINGS FROM THE CASE STUDIES SERIES

Bruce Trigger, *The Huron: Farmers of the North*. Chapters 5 and 6 introduce the principles of matriliny and matrilocality. The Huron are a well-known example of these principles, yet Trigger shows how important variation occurs in Huron social organization and suggests reasons for the changes.

Philip Newman, *Knowing the Gururumba*. Chapters 1, 2, and 3 show a similar variation for peoples usually described as patrilineal. Together with Trigger's case study, it provides a useful introduction to unilineal organization.

Edward Dozier, *The Kalinga of Northern Luzon, Philippines*. Chapter 1 is sufficient to indicate the similarities between cognatic descent groups and unilineal descent groups.

OTHER READINGS

Robin Fox, *Kinship and Marriage*. Fox analyzes the various types of kinship organization introduced in the preceding chapter, and he provides far more depth than can be offered here.

3

Cognatic Descent

Kinship is so much more systematic than politics, religion, or other social institutions that anthropologists have long worked at categorizing the different forms. Taxonomies of kinship systems began with Lewis Morgan's initial study of the field (1870), and classification continues today. This chapter represents one step in such classification and attempts to survey cognatic or bilateral systems in contrast to unilineal systems.

It is necessary, however, to emphasize the considerable variability that exists between two or more systems; indeed, variation occurs even within a single community. Homer Barnett (1960:51) makes this point very well in an introduction to Palauan social organization. He notes Palauans are not interested in kinship as such but see it as a vehicle for manipulating wealth.

> They use kinship and seek means to extend artificially its ramifications because it is only within this framework that they can contrive the wealth displays that bring prestige and influence. Kinship is, in fact, phrased in terms, not of friendship or affection or social solidarity, but of status and power.

Barnett compares kinship to a legal system that becomes a device for achieving personal success; one plays it up or down, demanding an obligation be filled but avoiding corresponding responsibility. The game may even be extended by treating nonrelatives like kin and making kinship demands of them. Thus a farsighted man chooses his relatives carefully, at least some of them. This observation from the South Seas closely parallels one made in the Mediterranean by Jeremy Boissevain (1969:14), who tells us in *Hal-Farrug: A Village in Malta* that villagers' social structure is not so much a reflection of values and norms but, rather, more a result of dozens of individual choices guided not only by norms but also by practicalities relating to the way an individual is playing the game. Choices are made not just in response to "What is expected of me by others?" but also in regard to "What is best for me and my family?" or even "How much can I get away with?"

It seems likely that people "get away with" more where descent is bilateral and kinship obligations are rigid only among nuclear family members. Leeway increases in direct proportion to the distance in degree of relationship. Without a descent group one is not bound to the rules of the membership, and one exercises considerable choice in establishing ties with other groups. A number of similarities in practice will occur in such circumstances, but these practices will vary from community to community. To illustrate the similarity and difference let us look first at five cases. For marked contrast we start with a Tibetan people and move to Japan, where modern urban conditions make some Japanese very familiar to us. Generally, of course, other Indo-European peoples are most like us, but some village groups have practices less familiar than the Japanese. The two villages we will look at in this context are in Malta and Greece. We then move on to survey a Colombian town whose people have a kinship system much like our own. These communities will then be compared to two communities in Borneo whose descent groups are based on cognatic descent. Such a distribution indicates the widespread distribution of cognatic descent, and its existence in a variety of economic or ecological contexts.

TIBETANS, COGNATIC DESCENT AMONG PASTORALISTS

Tibetan peoples generally are assumed to be organized into patrilineages. Not only do the Chinese on the north and the Indians on the south have traditional unilineal descent, but ruling patrilineal dynasties of Tibetans are well known. Robert Ekvall (1968:28) provides our ethnography of an isolated, nomadic Tibetan group in *Fields on the Hoof: Nexus of Tibetan Nomadic Pastoralism.* In it he assumes that lineage organization is characteristic, but for his community the lineage is "somewhat amorphous" or like "a clan in the process of decay." Such a group gathers only infrequently for a few ceremonies of a military character. In fact, then, the kinship structure is at the nuclear and extended family level.

According to Ekvall (1968:24) ownership of stock determines much of the tenor of Tibetan life. The pastoralist has a feeling of assured ownership that a farmer or peasant can never have, for the herds, or "fields on the hoof," have what Ekvall calls "elusiveness." This guarantees the owner that tax officials will find it more difficult to confiscate his moving "field" than land. Such a condition endows the Tibetan pastoralist with independence, a quality he values and ties to his capability for ownership.

This ownership lies essentially within the household, or more aptly the *tenthold.* The tenthold is typically a nuclear family, although sons ideally stay with their fathers throughout life. The father or eldest male manages the tenthold, making the decisions on herd management, links with the community, and disposal of herd products. Yet all family members have some ownership rights that may lead them to question the elder's leadership. The questioning most often arises from a wife. Frequently, it is the wife of a son who cannot coexist with a mother-in-law who is responsible for fragmentation of an extended family. Indeed, the extended form is best seen as a temporary stage in a cycle. Upon marriage a son brings home his bride, and a nuclear family becomes extended until he sets up a new tenthold. A younger brother may again "extend" the family temporarily when he marries. The breakoff of a married son is accomplished comparatively easily because of the nature of Tibetan property: Whereas fields cannot be easily divided, "fields on the hoof" can be. As soon as a son receives his share of the herd, he and his wife are ready to establish an independent tenthold. The "breakup" is also of ease because the couple is likely to remain in the same encampment, where they may expect reciprocal help.

As siblings marry and leave the tenthold, each takes an equal share in the herd. There is neither *primogeniture* to favor the eldest nor *ultimogeniture* to favor the youngest; nor is there a difference in inheritance of stock between sons and daughters. These Tibetans do see that half the herd belongs to the parents; the remaining half will be shared equally among the children. At the death of the parents their property ideally is consumed in religious observances, such as offerings to monasteries; actually, much of it passes on to the children.

The Tibetan sense of property allows a few cases of polygyny among the affluent. If a man marries two sisters or a mother and daughter, they may coexist in the same tenthold as a rare form of extended family. The usual polygynous practice though is to establish different tentholds for each wife. Ekvall tells us that no man "in his senses" would try to put two nonrelated women in the same tent. Women sharing the same tenthold may quarrel about control over the churn and its products, and they may even argue over sexual jealousies. Although rare, the polygynous household is generally stable, perhaps an indication that individuals capable of two marriages exert particularly strong control.

A polyandrous form of marriage accounts for another extended family form. The two or more men sharing a wife are usually brothers, and such an arrangement allows them to stay in one tent with one tent mistress. Most importantly, the male siblings keep the herd intact and display a greater wealth than usual. In this case, sexual jealousy can also occur, and as the wife begins to favor one brother over the other, the scorned man looks elsewhere. He, of course, takes his share of the herd when he finds a wife.

The economics of Tibetan ownership account for another variation of extended family: In a tent lacking a son, a man may well persuade the man who marries his daughter to reside with him. Affluent families without sons commonly take in a poorer husband for their daughter, and the son-in-law becomes a surrogate son.

This latter case sometimes occurs among ourselves for quite similar reasons. Indeed, all the Tibetan practices are not too foreign to us, even with their polygyny and polyandry. Perhaps the greatest difference between us lies in the precedence of economics over sanctioned sex and protection of children. Ekvall (1968:27) suggests several reasons for these differences.

> There is a considerable degree of sexual license . . . and satisfaction is not dependent on formally sanctioned arrangements . . . there is a dearth of children. . . . An unmarried mother is, if anything, more desirable than one without children and adoption of children by childless families takes place frequently.

There is only the suggestion of an organization beyond the nuclear and extended families. Tibetans recognize a group they call *TSHo Ba*, which seems to be a lineage or clan, but it is of little importance. As noted earlier, Ekvall dismisses it as a decaying clan.

In sum, peoples in far-off Tibet share a number of similarities with us because they organize their households on the basis of cognatic descent. Herds can be managed quite effectively by the household; they are broken up each generation and passed on to both sons and daughters. No larger groups have formed, nor do they seem necessary, to control the herds. If one were to substitute "money" for "herds" in the above sentences, the generalizations could apply just as well to the American family.

JAPAN, URBANISM AND COGNATIC DESCENT

Let us now turn to another family type in which money is indeed becoming the major form of property as a result of industrialization and urban life; our case is Japan. Edward Norbeck (1965) provides the appropriate ethnography through the case study of a family in *Changing Japan*. The husband of this family was born into a traditional rural household, which he shared with many siblings and a grandmother. He was almost adopted by his father's sister who lived nearby. Like most rural Japanese the extended family was all-important for him, and the extension tended to follow agnatic links.

When the husband-to-be, Jiro, finished the sixth grade as an outstanding student, his relatives urged him to attend high school for several reasons: Older brothers were taking over the father's tasks, there was little room for Jiro, and education was valued as a means of achievement. When the family had decided on this course for Jiro, they banded together to use kinship and personal ties to contact the high-school principal. While Jiro attended high school, his kin took pride in his accomplishment, and Jiro remained close to them, but new vistas of the world began to open, even if only through books.

When Jiro graduated near the top of his class, his parents had in mind his marriage into a prominent family having only daughters. Although men are advised against such a practice, it is a practical way for a poor Japanese boy "to make good" just as it is for a Tibetan or American. Jiro's aunt, however, had different plans and steered Jiro toward the university. With the death of her husband, she built a new life that included Jiro's education. After a Spartan existence at a highly competitive university, Jiro entered the business world. The Asahi firm employed him at what seemed very high wages and liberal benefits, but with his rural backgroud they were unlikely to promote him to a higher position. Jiro's tastes quickly increased to match his income, and money problems continued. He was unable to set aside much for his aunt or parents, and when he returned home he found relations estranged. Jiro was no longer part of his village.

Back in the city Jiro continued at his work and impressed a supervisor who encouraged him to study law. When Jiro successfully completed exams for patent law, his employer again approached him with another proposal: Would he take a wife? At twenty-seven Jiro was finally ready for marriage. It had been postponed much longer than his father's marriage, and, whereas that marriage had been arranged by relatives, Jiro's was being arranged by an employer.

Aki, the girl picked for Jiro, came from a well-to-do family living in an Osaka suburb. She had learned all the social graces and had finished college at a Christian mission without any intent of ever converting to Christianity. Upon graduation at twenty-two, her parents had planned a marriage for her. To their surprise Aki rejected two early prospects and four later ones. Many older Japanese saw Aki as a hopeless old maid at twenty-seven, but she continued to speak of marriage without any rush toward it. When she met Jiro, she recognized another progressive young modern. Although the two objected to a formal arranged marriage in the traditional manner, they began "to date" much like Westerners. After a few months they married, honeymooned, and settled into married life.

At this point their life became remarkably like that of many urban Americans. After a brief sojourn with Aki's parents, the couple began the round of apartment hunting. The tiny one they found in the suburbs took much of Jiro's salary and commuting took much of his time. Aki soon was managing the finances and, as very often happens, began spending more than Jiro made. Financially her mother secretly helped, but when Aki became pregnant, she realized they must find housing within their means. With luck, they found government housing and moved into a high-rise. The cheaper quarters allowed full independence from parents, and Aki and Jiro adapted to instant foods and became progressive, more cautious, television viewers as well as book readers, and installment buyers. In short, they were solid middle class.

After the birth of the baby and Jiro's slow rise in business, this family's career continued to resemble the American family. Jiro was well on his way toward becoming an "organization man." He and Aki, like many other urban Japanese, were wrapped up solely in a nuclear family, turning only occasionally to members of their kindred for help or an infrequent visit. Relatives outside the nuclear family were not spurned; there simply was no time for them.

This remote Japanese family is perhaps too close to us in structure to allow full appreciation of variation. Of course, it is important to realize how much like us quite different people can be, but here, when we are interested in variation on a theme, it will be useful to look at the countryside. Two Mediterranean cases supply a perspective. Jeremy Boissevain (1969) writes that Maltese islanders in the village of Farrug believe a household should be composed of nuclear family members. (You may note that the Japanese did not seem to regard it so much as an ideal as a necessity.) Yet reality differs considerably from cultural expectation. In a number of households grown children had emigrated or married; even more commonly a household accommodated other relatives. Less than half the households lived up to the ideal.

HAL-FARRUG, COGNATIC DESCENT WITH MATRILATERAL BIAS

Ideals about family roles, however, are more likely to be realized because religious sanctions control much of family life. Incorrect role performance is subject to notice by the Catholic Church as well as public opinion. The prescribed role of the husband/father is to provide and exercise authority, and that of the wife/mother is to produce and train children. Maltese law further enforces these sex-typed roles, and it seems most Maltese do accept such differences in status as God-given; few consciously question the subordination of women to men.

This subordination pattern could probably continue if Maltese did indeed live in nuclear families, but fundamental change makes their ideal difficult to achieve. Malta is becoming industrialized, and each year fewer families in Hal-Farrug are full-time agriculturists. As a farming unit the husband/father had to direct the family activity, yet as children go to different industrial jobs they leave the direction of their father. In addition, a child may support his parents by sending money to his mother. More and more Maltese women are coming to control more of the purse; some even manage an income of their own.

Furthermore, the authority of the father works to undermine male authority in the full cycle of family growth. Parents and children are traditionally close, but, as they mature, the father's authority becomes a burden particularly to sons. Daughters, on the other hand, grow closer to their mothers, and, by the time she marries, a woman has become a cooperating partner with her mother and desires to stay nearby. Men, however, are ready to break with their fathers and are willing to settle in their brides' neighborhood. Statistically, then, the people of Hal-Farrug are matrilocal, although norms of residence do not exist.

Norms about relationships define the kindred as important but clearly as only secondary in importance to the nuclear family. Kindred generally see each other weekly and share mutual rights and obligations, but distance diminishes contact and reciprocal sharing. Affines or relatives by marriage are also important, and when an individual marries, he acquires many more affines. Father's brother's wife is much like the "aunt" we are familiar with, and the wife's brother may be especially close. Brothers-in-law often share and cooperate more than brothers.

Of course, it is not possible to maintain the same degree of contact with this myriad of kin; an individual Maltese limits his kin contact to a small percentage of the total. Boissevain (1969:23) notes that distinctions between affines and consanguines can be made by Maltese, but in day-to-day life, "The categories of relatives form a *network* of relations and not separate groups. A person chooses a set of relatives out of his total network of relatives." To understand the behavior of any one individual it is necessary to determine what network he has established.

Individual choice, then, is significant in the formation of functional kin groups. Yet a picture of such Maltese groups reveals a pattern. Does the pattern result from a bias toward the patrilateral or matrilateral relatives? From the above brief introduction to Maltese you should be able to answer this question.

If you are not certain of your answer, recall that Hal-Farrug families tend toward matrilocality. A woman's tie to her mother brings the groom in touch with wife's brothers, at least those who are not living in the distant village of the wife. As children are born they tend to be in more contact with their maternal rather than paternal grandparents. Boissevain notes further that a couple often resides with a widowed parent or bachelor brother. In the latter case, incest regulations eliminate any sexual competition between a husband and his wife's brother, whereas competition could arise if the couple came to live with a bachelor brother of the groom. The Maltese conditions with their matrilateral bias lead to a special relation with the mother's brother, an unusual occurrence for a bilateral society.

This relationship is not so structured, however, that it is built into everyone's network of relationships. It must be emphasized that the availability of choice in Maltese kinship allows considerable variation and adaptability and even allows inclusion of nonrelatives in the network. Still, village conditions have brought some regularity to network formations.

VASILIKA, COGNATIC DESCENT WITH PATRILATERAL BIAS

A Greek village offers us an interesting contrast to the Maltese. In general outline, conditions are much the same, and family life is quite similar except for a patrilateral bias in the networks. A brief review of Ernestine Friedl's (1962) ethnography indicates the reasons for the Greek differences. *Vasilika: A Village in Modern Greece* describes an agricultural community where all available land is farmed. Greek tradition and law call for equal division of property, most of it land, among all children. Yet villagers recognize (1962:49) that further division of the land would soon result in uneconomical plots. Thus daughters receive their share of the property in the form of a *dowry*. Villagers understand very well that the dowry is a girl's share of the family's wealth and only incidentally part of marriage. It is useful in marriage to indicate to the groom what wealth he may expect. When his *patrimony* equals roughly the bride's dowry, negotiations are fairly simple (1962:54). The dowry is largely household furnishings but frequently consists of land as well. A man's patrimony is always land, and a couple will reside upon it. Since most villages are small and kinship is bilateral, supplemented with psuedo-kinship ties of godparenthood, a girl must marry outside her village. This village exogamy leads to patrilocal residence, though the bride's land may keep her and her husband in close touch with her home village for some years. In some cases, an outsider appears to be performing bride service in Vasilika because of his wife's landholding. In actuality, however, this plot eventually will be exchanged for one nearer the groom's village.

The brothers who remain on their father's farm begin to encounter problems (1962:60) as they marry. Their wives become especially jealous of each other after the death of the parents and the birth of children. The brothers are hesitant to break apart because the land will be fractionated, and new household expenses must be borne. Inevitably, measures are taken to alter the living arrangements. In some cases where only two brothers are involved, they may simply divide their original home with a wall sufficient to separate the living quarters. Where new houses must be built, they may cooperate in building and then hold a lottery to determine who gets which house. They must also increase their holdings or send out "extra" brothers.

Several generations ago Vasilikans recognized this problem and began to reduce family size. Improved health conditions led to population increase, however. One solution was to educate a son for city life so, like Jiro in Japan, a number of Vasilikans left for Athens. The expense of an education was reckoned part of the patrimony. Once before many other sons emigrated to America, and today a Tanzanian emigrant is known as "the American." All in all the Vasilikans manage to keep the farm plots at an economical size.

As you should be aware, the patrilocal residence, which is common to Vasilika, favors a network established among the husband/father's relatives; Vasilika is, therefore, a converse of the Maltese village. Another subtle difference arises in concepts about the marriage tie. The Greeks see marriage as allying two nuclear families and not just bride and groom. Kinship terms reflect the concept very well, and special terms are reserved for doubling binding ties when two brothers marry two sisters. This concept of alliance is long familiar to anthropology and will be discussed later. It probably was once integral to Greek marriage but has dwindled with increasing emphasis on the nuclear family. One final problem arises from this Greek case. If males inherit land from their fathers and pass it to their sons, why don't perpetual property-owning groups arise? That is, why are patrilineages absent from the Greek countryside?

Friedl (1962:64) provides several answers. Her major one is that the division of land is so extensive and land trades or purchases are so common that no estates develop that could be associated with lineages. Since emphasis remains on bilateral descent and the nuclear family, the Greek family resembles our own. However, an even more similar organization is to be found in San Pedro, Colombia, where life is very much like Mainstreet, U.S.A., according to Miles Richardson (1970:20) in his case study, *San Pedro, Colombia: Small Town in a Developing Society.*

SAN PEDRO, COGNATIC DESCENT IN THE DEVELOPING COUNTRYSIDE

San Pedro's 200 families make it larger than a village, a small town perhaps. Only one-quarter of the family heads are agriculturists. A chicken industry, cigar making, and a small factory for billiard cues involve San Pedro directly in the national economy and require close urban ties. San Pedranos are Colombians in much the way Podunkans are Americans, and like their counterparts they have a bullfight that parallels minor-league baseball and a Chicken Queen much like a Strawberry Queen. They also have some pride in small town life unlike rural peasants who are convinced city life must always be better.

In this small town a semblance of industrialization has allowed an independence that in turn led to an increasing number of nuclear families. Moreover, in this Latin culture the well-entrenched ideas of male dominance and superiority have given way to real behavior that allows female equality and even superordination. Richardson (1970:86) reports more than a fifth of the families as "matriarchal" or headed by females and adds that in other households women may have the ultimate word.

The partner who has the last word seems closely tied to economics. Women are important if they own the house or have an outside job. Their production and income are valued, and men are willing to share authority in return. Men are quick to take advantage of other economic opportunity as well; in this, they do not let extended kin hamper their style. The kindred may give some support in youth, but its value diminishes with maturity unless a relative is in a position to be of special help. He, of course, will play the game to avoid giving help. In place of extended kin or kindred, San Pedranos make use of the pseudo-ties of *compadrazco* or godparenthood. Such kin are important among Maltese and Greeks, but there the institution seems clearly to supplement other forms of kinship. In San Pedro, however, *compadre* relations seem to replace real kin ties. A man asks a wealthy landowner or urbanite to sponsor his child's baptism or wedding. The sponsor becomes godfather or *padrino* to the child; he becomes a *compadre* of the parent. *Compadres* can make considerable demands upon each other, and in many cases the relation parallels that of client–patron. The wealthy *compadre* furnishes loans in crises, steers bright godchildren to school, and intervenes with tax collectors or other officials. In turn, the poor *compadre* is ready to furnish labor or political support and to spread kind words and praise about his *compadre* in the town. The use of the relationship is truly indicative of the San Pedranos' practicality and eagerness "to get ahead."

These townsmen are also knit to Colombian society through national politics and the Catholic Church. Ties of this sort have replaced the kind of networks that exist in Vasilika. Instead, a person has networks in a variety of systems: the political, the economic, the religious, and the institution of *compadrazco*. Kin relations revolve almost solely around the nuclear family, and Richardson (1970:89–90) describes families as

> irreducible social cells, whose outer, protective husk is the house. . . . membership . . . stops at the front door. . . . participation in the familial institutions turns them inward, toward the intimate world of their wives, husbands, sons, and daughters.

This family system of San Pedro is illustrated by a case study of Seneca, a young man about to marry. Richardson (1970:79) offers us a picture of a man with ambitions like Jiro. Seneca has acquired a better-than-average education and has moved on to improved work. Presently he is close to his mother and other family, but one suspects strongly that after marriage he may move into the city and lose touch with his siblings.

This migration is a process that is accelerated in Japan and San Pedro but is also important on Malta and is evident in Vasilika. Indeed, it is a worldwide process and must have begun some five thousand years ago with the urban revolution. The pattern probably started with some children of a family leaving for the city, a journey whose physical distance cuts social ties markedly. It is difficult to see how corporate kin groups could be maintained in such a process. Not only does the city draw people out of the village, but its influences have increasingly infiltrated into village life. Villages no longer simply produce a food surplus, for their ambitions have grown with the economy. Villagers are asked, or many times they themselves ask, to become part of the industrial world. In Hal-Farrug, for example, small-time capitalists operated a bus company; San Pedro had a cigar and billiard cue factory. Wage employment brings ready property fragmentations, it often changes sex and age roles, and almost always the potential for migration markedly increases. All these factors operate to reduce extended kin ties and to maximize the importance of the nuclear family. Thus the nuclear family is the primary kin unit in communities that are part of the urban world. As the Tibetan case shows, the nuclear family may be equally important under other conditions as well.

Given nuclear family life, the mother and father have all-embracing roles, and children are tied strongly to both of them. Ties to both sides, or bilateral descent, logically follows. Formerly anthropologists assumed that bilateral descent limited kinship organization to the nuclear or extended family. The case studies above offer support for such an interpretation. However, more extensive research in Southeast Asia, summarized by George Murdock (1960), indicated that descent groups can and do form where descent is cognatic or bilateral. Anthropologists have suggested a variety of terms for such groups, such as *ramage, ambilineal descent group*, and *non-unilineal descent group*, as well as bilateral descent group. *Cognatic descent group* will be employed here in place of these other terms.

PADJU EPAT, COGNATIC DESCENT GROUPS

A useful example of a cognatic descent group will be drawn from the island of Borneo. Many different peoples have occupied Borneo and a range of social organization abounds on the island. The type of organization that most interests us here can be found in the province of Central Kalimantan. Alfred Hudson (1972) describes in *Padju Epat: The Ma'anyan of Indonesian Borneo* a community whose people shift residence often and form new hamlets around different farm fields. Moreover, the Padju Epater is said to crave variety and desires a near yearly change in neighbors and domicile. Of course, kinship groups remain fairly stable, and composition of the *dangau*, or nuclear family, changes slowly. The *lewu'*, or extended family grouping, is also stable, but its composition reflects the variety that is available to these Borneo people. The *lewu'* extended kin is often a daughter-in-law or son-in-law. Significantly, a man locates with his wife's parents about as often as a woman locates with her husband's parents. Although choice of residence is open at the time of marriage, postmarital residence is expected to be stable. The actual physical place of residence will shift, of course, but a couple is expected to stay with the *lewu'* family of first choice.

This much stability seems an essential ingredient for any agricultural society, where arable land must be allocated on a fairly regular basis. The tie between land and family is clear from *adat* (tradition or customary law), which governs the Padju Epat; moreover, the tie seems fundamental in forming an even larger kin group, called the *bumuh*. The *bumuh* is a cognatic descent group, and its features are worth describing in some depth. Hudson's interest in *adat* law and land rights (1972:84) leads to such a description.

Rights to land go to the individual who first clears virgin forest. Let us call him a "pioneer" with "pioneer use rights." He passes on such rights equally to sons and daughters, but, as elsewhere, some heirs become "more equal" than others. Let us suppose that a pioneer cleared more than enough land for himself and has two sons and a daughter. When two of the children marry, they and their spouses can work the land, but one heir will need to settle with his or her spouse. Neither *adat* law nor Padju Epat norms direct which of the heirs shall stay after marriage. Most likely, whichever of the three spouses has the most land will take one of the heirs to his or her hamlet. The out-marrying heir maintains a share in the estate, but it is not as significant as the shares controlled by those who use the land. As use of land became complicated, it was necessary for one of the heirs to direct its use. Let us assume that one of the male heirs moved to his wife's hamlet; of the remaining brother and sister, the brother allocated the land, keeping in mind his brother's interest. This brother became custodian of the land, and the custodianship would become an inherited position. Any of his children could inherit; his sister's children were also potential heirs. A succession line of custodians with relatives tied to it through both male and female links emerges. The original founder will be forgotten eventually, but descendants orient themselves to a line of custodians.

A number of prerequisites determines custodianship, but sex is not one of them. Obviously, a good memory is, for an individual must be able to recall recent predecessors and how people are linked to this line. Rights to land and other *bumuh* property are loaned, given, or otherwise exchanged so a custodian also must keep track of numerous *bumuh* transactions and memorize an inventory of property and tradition.

The rights in a *bumuh* are closely matched to responsibilities. *Adat* law specifies three degrees of rights: Primary rights go to heirs who remain part of their parents' household; secondary rights go to children who chose another household but remained within the hamlet; tertiary rights are held by heirs who married in a different hamlet. Children with primary rights carry full responsibility for parents in old age; if there are no such children, then persons with secondary rights must assume the care.

Rights accrue at the beginning of an agricultural season when farm plots are selected. As families select land, they inform their *bumuh* custodian. Generally, individuals have a good idea who will select what land, but when two individuals do select the same site, their order of rights will determine settlement of the claim. Presently, virgin lands are still available for clearing, and few complex cases of land claims arise. Under such conditions *bumuh* membership works well in establishing and maintaining land rights.

Sites within the forest are casually marked by clusters of fruit trees. These trees began unintentionally when a family lived on the land and discarded seeds of the fruit it ate. The trees remained long after the hut was abandoned and had disappeared, because mature fruit trees are not cut when preparing the new fields. In time majestic fruit trees mark *bumuh* property as well as become part of it. Thus a Padju Epater, when asked about his rights to a tract of land, may point to a grove of trees and say, "Those are the remains of my wife's grandfather's occupancy, and we get our rights from him."

Other types of trees and property comprise more of the *bumuh* estate, but significantly rubber trees do not. They are owned by individuals, and when a man wants to plant rubber trees, he must get permission to use *bumuh* land. This act removes the land from *bumuh* use for fifty or more years or even permanently. The plantation becomes, in effect, private property, and individuals have sold such land without consulting the *bumuh* custodian. Likewise, other possessions acquired by individual effort remain individual property. A ceremonial sword, for instance, does not become *bumuh* property.

Some individuals, on the other hand, do build up a collection of such items. Bronze gongs, brass trays, and Chinese ceramics may form an heirloom collection that has value *as a collection*. The collector will not want to see items dispersed to heirs; therefore, he transfers the property to a custodian, and descendants have an undivided interest in the heirloom collection. This case suggests what the nature of property may be when it is held by a corporate group such as a cognatic descent group.

The difficulty with cognatic descent is that relatives multiply like rabbits. There are two parents, four grandparents, and eight great-grandparents; in ten generations there are 1024 ancestors, and descendants multiply on the same scale. Unilineal descent wipes out so many of the ancestors that descent groups remain on a manageable scale. How can people follow cognatic descent and achieve the same end? The answer is simple and extremely practical: Remember only those relatives who can further your goals. An individual wishing to claim D.A.R. membership may follow the links to a colonial patriot and ignore those that lead to a Tory scoundrel or a neutral war profiteer. Under cognatic descent the rules of the game encourage much choice; under unilineal descent the rules demand that each male ancestor (or female ancestress) be remembered. How much more practical is cognatic descent! It allows greater opportunity to claim greatness and to avoid meanness.

DUSUN, ENDOGAMOUS COGNATIC DESCENT GROUPS

To avoid further embarrassment we may pass over our own practices at this point and look at the Dusun, another Borneo people. Thomas Rhys Williams in *The Dusun: A North Borneo Society* (1965:48) describes a group, the *senAkAgun*, which closely resembles the *bumuh*. All members of a *senAkAgun* claim a common ancestor. Note that only one particular ancestor is claimed, and his activities are preserved in legend and folktale. Perhaps most importantly, land is owned in his name. A person who wishes to share in the use of this land must establish an ancestor tie through *either* parent or any of the grandparents, very much like the people of Padju Epat. We do not know for certain if there is a definite correlation between the amount of land connected to an ancestor and the number of ties that are established to him, but the trend is probably in that direction.

The land around Sensuron is associated with the ancestor *tohau*. Not surprisingly, nearly every Sensuron villager claims *tohau* as an ancestor. Moreover, many other villages join with Sensuron in claiming *tohau* as their founding ancestor. A large population is necessary for the *senAkAgun* because this cognatic descent group is endogamous. An occasional marriage outside the group is permitted, but special ritual must sanction it. Clearly such marriages are regarded as potentially troublesome because the *senAkAgun* not only owns land but also trees, jars, gongs, weapons, and ritual paraphernalia. Since individual members are allowed to use this group porperty, and females as well as males have *usufruct rights*, any marriage to an outsider permits the outsider to exert claims through the spouse.

Since internal claims cause sufficient problems for the Dusun, outsiders are seldom welcome. Given the large size of Dusun descent groups, internal conflicts are to be expected on a large scale. As you might anticipate, a people who are flexible in establishing descent group membership are also flexible in choosing leaders. Each village of the *tohau* descent group has a village headman whose powers derive from the founding ancestor. However, this power goes to the one who demonstrates that he can force agreement to a settlment among disputing villagers. These headmen, in turn, meet to select one *tohau* leader. One Dusun says (1965:50) that the *tohau* leader is "so smart that when he talks people are afraid of him."

That is, he can force all *tohau* members into agreement. He takes precedence over village headmen in ritual and adjudication of intervillage disputes, and he may also rally *tohau* members in economic and political matters.

In the villages around Sensuron the descent groups control land tenure without question; even when cash crops are planted, the land and income remain in the hands of the descent group. However Sensuron is experiencing change. These villagers have begun intensive irrigation of rice, and, like the rubber trees of Padju Epat, the rice lands and irrigation systems are in the possession of nuclear families. Furthermore, a number of gongs, jars, and beads are now owned by families instead of descent groups. Williams suggests that more land is always available in the hills for dry rice farming, and the descent group can easily furnish its members with such land. In Sensuron, where the demand for wet rice land is intense, individual ownership has solved the problem of competition. This interpretation seems likely, but compare it to Chapter 2's description of what happened among the Kalinga of the Philippines. What was the difference there between wet rice and dry rice farmers? Under intensive wet rice farming among the Kalinga, cognatic descent groups seemed to be developing, whereas the same wet rice farming among the Dusun suggests a diminishing importance for the descent group. How might you account for such a discrepancy?

On the basis simply of Dusun and Kalinga, you have little chance of discovering the answer. You might consult more technical works of the two authors, but, even then, you may not find a satisfactory solution. I would suggest that the Kalinga irrigation systems are on a greater scale than those of the Dusun. The former support, or even demand, a large self-perpetuating membership, which controls the property, whereas the Dusun systems are only large enough to support a nuclear family. Moreover, the latter have been in existence such a short time that corporate descent groups have not had time to form around the irrigation. The already existing corporate groups are simply too large for fields to be shared among the members.

At any rate, this problem is of less importance, for our purposes, than your understanding of how cognatic descent groups form. In many respects, such a group is very much like a lineage or a unilineal descent group. Indeed, it could have been included in the next chapter. It is described here, however, because it is based on bilateral descent, just as are most societies in which only the nuclear and/or extended family are the basis for kinship organization.

You might note a further similarity among the Greek and Maltese villages and Padju Epat and the Dusun. Given the choice available in these kinship systems, the *network* established in Hal-Farrug or Vasilika is much like the cognatic descent group. Although networks usually vary for each individual, a prominent person is often the "target" for numerous living people. When they "reach" him, they have established a tenuous link among themselves. The process resembles the one used in Borneo; people with cognatic descent groups simply consider the links a much more binding tie, and they generally establish more important functions for such a group.

When the group becomes so important it cannot be allowed to "die" with the death of its membership, it begins to resemble a lineage because of its "corporate-ness." Corporate groups, ones that go on in perpetuity, exist in almost all societies. We first think of business corporations as corporate groups, but the Presbyterian Church, Cook County, the Boy Scouts, and Yale University are also corporate groups. In the next chapter, we will discover that whereas we entrust economic, religious, political, and educational matters to large, impersonal bureaucratic corporations, other communities invest these things in corporate kin groups. One possibility, of course, is the cognatic descent group, but the common form of corporate kin group is a unilineal descent group.

EXERCISES

1. Consult the first three chapters in *Hal-Farrug* to understand better the ways in which a network of social relations is established largely through kinship lines but altered significantly by occupation or ownership of property. Then compare Maltese to the Florida community of hippies in William Partridge's case study, *The Hippie Ghetto*. Chapter 2 describes a network among hippies formed largely on shared values and occupation, but even here some kinship links remain basic. The similarity between the network formations in the two communities is striking.

2. Return to the kinship diagram you constructed for yourself in Chapter 1. What network would you pick out from among these relatives? What would be your criteria for determining inclusion and exclusion of relatives? Some possi-bilities are amount of visiting, mutual aid, affect, and help in times of stress. How can some of these factors be made objective? What other persons would you want to include in your network? Are most of them peers? If you list persons from another generation, do the criteria for their inclusion differ from those for peers?

SUGGESTED READINGS FROM THE CASE STUDIES SERIES

Jeremy Boissevain, *Hal-Farrug: A Village in Malta*. The first three chapters introduce a specific case of bilateral descent and the topic of networks. The description further illustrates how people frequently manipulate their kinship systems.

A. B. Hudson, *Padju Epat: The Ma'anyan of Indonesian Borneo*. The manipulation of descent ties to form cognatic descent groups is documented fully in Chapters 8 through 12. On the one hand, this ethnography suggests that a conscious process is important in determining the descent group; on the other hand, it strongly suggests that kin groups are a product of adaptation to a particular environment.

4
Unilineal Descent

As noted in Chapter 2 unilineal descent makes a great deal of "sense" to us, even though, as Westerners, we have experienced only cognatic descent principles. Corporate groups based on kinship are unlikely in the cognatic descent-based society, but they do occur, as in the Philippine highlands and the Borneo mountains. In cases of unilineal descent, descent groups are almost inevitable, and these groups have much in common, whether the links are male or female. With few exceptions, where unilineal descent groups are found, most economic, political, and religious organization centers on them. In short, if they exist, they are essential.

In the early years of anthropology, theorists saw matriliny as a stage for the later development of patriliny. When we assumed one had developed out of the other, it followed that the latter would be more complex. As theorists moved away from the concept of evolution, they began to perceive the many similarities among unilineal descent groups everywhere. Most recently, we have begun to recognize that differences between matriliny and patriliny do indeed occur, but they arise because of overt male control rather than evolutionary change.

From a survey of unilineal descent groups presented in this chapter, I am going to ask you first to deduce a list of characteristics common to all descent groups. After this exercise, we will look further at these cases in order to derive generalizations about differences between patriliny and matriliny. In the process I will also be pointing out some differences among matrilineal peoples and another range of differences among patrilineal societies. (Recall from Chapter 2 that the differences among the former are somewhat greater than the latter.)

The ethnographic cases for matriliny are written by Keith Basso (1970) and Edward Dozier (1966). Basso writes of *The Cibecue Apache,* and Dozier (also writer of the Kalinga case study) describes *Hano: A Tewa Indian Community in Arizona.* Cases of patriliny are available also from the four corners of the world. Louis Faron (1968) has written of *The Mapuche Indians of Chile,* Evon Vogt (1970) of *The Zinacantecos of Mexico,* William Bascom (1969) of *The Yoruba of Southwestern Nigeria,* John Beattie (1960) of *Bunyoro* in East Africa, and Leopold Pospisil (1963) of *The Kapauku Papuans of West New Guinea.* We will begin with the matrilineal communities.

HANO, MATRILINY WITH FIXED AUTHORITY

The Hopi Indians of Arizona have served anthropologists as the classic case of matriliny. Their social organization readily compares with other pueblo Indians in Arizona and New Mexico, and the pueblos reflect a wide range of social organization described by Fred Eggan (1950) in a valuable theoretical study. For our purposes we may turn to one of the many pueblos on the Hopi mesas, that of Hano. Its people are latecomers among the Hopi and speak a distinctive language known as Tewa. Legend confirms what is linguistic evidence for a comparatively recent migration, probably an escape from early Spanish domination. Hano social organization apparently changed quickly to resemble that of the Hopi, even though they preserved their language and a number of other traits.

We receive an insider's view of Hano because Dozier himself was a pueblo Indian. We can trust his judgment when he (1966:39) relates, "Married men live with their wives, but look upon the households of their mothers and sisters as their real homes." On a day-to-day basis a Tewa "lives in" at his wife's household, but he returns frequently to his natal household, where he is responsible for junior members and ceremonial manners. Although a typical household might often be composed of a nuclear family, its orientation is basically different. It centers on a woman and her maternal relatives. Frequently, when a family is extended the household will include the wife's brothers, sisters, or sisters' children. Of course, her mother may also be a member, whereas the husband's mother would never be part of a household except under most unusual circumstances.

In each household the oldest woman serves as a representative to the matrilineage. Among households, one woman is judged head of the lineage. Again, among a larger grouping of such households, one woman is judged a clan elder, a position whose influence enables her brother or her mother's brother to head a clan. As Dozier (1966:39) puts it, "Hano households are the terminal structures of a number of matrilineal lineages which in turn form the important clan structures. One household in each clan is the custodian of the ceremonial lore and the religious paraphernalia of the clan."

In the old pueblo the extended family occupied a series of contiguous rooms. Women owned the buildings, and the eldest directed activities and gave advice. Husbands of the women contributed to its economy but had very little authority even over their own children. They did provide warmth and affection, but in ceremonial instruction and discipline a man deferred to his wife's brothers. Under a wage economy this traditional household gives way to the isolated, nuclear family household, but easy access among pueblo dwellers still allows extended family members to congregate along former lines.

Contact with father's relatives is also frequent and easy because Hano is not a large village. They provide affect like the father and also offer support in some of the more difficult ceremonials. The importance of father's relatives is such that one has special ties with his lineage.

One's own lineage is of utmost importance, however. Women of a lineage are in constant close association, while men return frequently to their lineage households. Regular ceremonial and ritual occasions bring lineage mates into intimate contact. So close are the ties among lineage and clan members that marriage must be out of this group, and this exogamous rule applies even to Hopi and Navajo clans of the same name. In addition to marriage, clans also regulate land use. Ownership of farm lands, as well as village sites, rests with the clan, and clan leaders vest usufruct or "use" rights in members. Ownership of ritual and ceremonial paraphernalia is likewise invested in the clans. With such responsibilities the Tewa must insure the perpetuity of clans. Although a few clans are recognized as extinct, the Tewa recognize links with Hopi clans of the same name and can perpetuate clan functions through appropriate Hopi or even other pueblo Indians.

These structural features of clan life are augmented by clan feelings well expressed by one of Dozier's (1966:42) informants:

> I am of the Bear clan. Our mothers' mothers' mothers and our mothers' mothers' mothers' brothers were Bear clan people. They came a long, long, time ago from . . . the east. Our sisters' daughters' daughters' children, as long as women of my clan have children, will be of the Bear clan. These are our clan relatives, whom we trust, work with, and confide in. My mother's older sister guards the sacred fetish. . . . [She] and my mother's brother make all the important decisions for our clan. . . .

Note how a diagram helps to understand the relations which this informant so readily perceives.

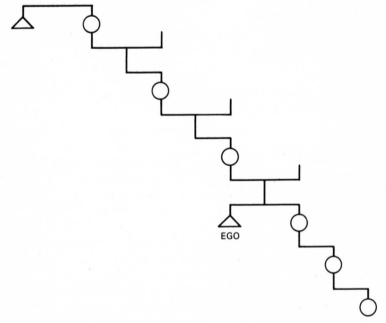

Figure 4A. Tewa model for a clan illustrating its perpetuity through females.

It is significant that Dozier completes his description of consanguine relations before examining husband–wife relations. Further, he discusses these relations under a section labeled "Life Cycle," rather than in the previous section on "Kinship Behavior." He tells us that relations between a Tewa husband and wife may be marked by deep affect after a long marriage and that the divorce rate of 20 percent is only half that of the Hopi. For a matrilineal people, the Tewa seem exceptional in their marital stability; even so, many marriages end in divorce. A man remains tied to the household of his sisters and mother throughout his life. He can allow only a partial attachment to his wife when so many duties take him back to his own lineage household. In concise terms, his father/husband status is limited by his mother's brother/brother status.

Just how much conflict results from these two statuses in a matrilineal society? If you will recall, Chapter 2 explored what happens with matrilocal peoples. A man must return often to his mother's household for his lineage duties, or he may assume authority in wife's household. Clearly for Hano a man returns to his mother. But will this pattern cause stress? Hano is unusual because of its small size, compactness, and location within a large group. A Tewa has the unusual opportunity of possibly returning to mother's simply by crossing the street. He also has an unusual closeness with his fellow Tewa because of the proximity of "outside" Hopi. Thus some of the inherent strains of matrilineal organization are present but modified.

CIBECUE APACHE, MATRILINY WITH SHIFTING AUTHORITY

In contrast, the Cibecue Apache live in much more scattered settlements. Prior to the reservation, households were even more scattered, and mobility was high. With peace, the Apache took up reservation life, but their homes remained apart and subtribal differences limited marriage choices.

One of five subtribal groups of the Western Apache, the Cibecue were further divided into bands. These bands, largely territorial units with no overall political organization, were further divided into local groups, again territorial units. Within the local group, however, there was complex political and economic organization. A chief headed each local unit and directed hunting and raiding expeditions as well as some farming operations. He also regulated relations with other groups. The local group had exclusive rights to its territory and was responsible for its defense.

From two to six extended families made up the local group. Matrilateral relatives were most likely to be added to the nuclear core with an elderly woman responsible for the household. A matrilocal rule prevailed, although a man would reside patrilocally if his mother or sisters needed a male in the household. Unlike the band which was strictly territorial, the local group was identified as kinship based. The core members of a matrilineage belonged to a larger clan, and each local group was identified by clan. Some members of the local group, the in-married males for example, did not belong to the clan with which they were identified. The Apache, of course, readily recognized who were and were not members, but for many purposes actual membership was only a technicality.

Although clan organization demanded clan exogamy, the Cibecue tended toward endogamy within band areas. The activities of both men and women demanded detailed knowledge of a territory; thus a man chose to marry as close to his local group as he could. Even so, conditions might take him to a camp a day's journey away, or shifting camps might separate him some distance from his mother and sisters.

While young, a man found himself in the position typical of matrilineal, matrilocal peoples. He was a stranger among his wife's clansmen and returned to his mother's for clan duties. Upon his return to his new residence, however, he gradually began to feel more at home, and distance diminished the ties to his natal group. Over time a man would develop authority in his home so that his wife's relatives might be considered living with him, rather than he with them. Headmen such as these were important in local level politics, making decisions about camp movement, internal disputes, and codes of morality.

In contrast, clan leadership provided for large-scale political organization, a necessity in Apache-type warfare, raiding, and defense. The clans of the Cibecue were similar to those of the Huron and Tewa in terms of being composed of matrilineages with leadership of each lineage and an overall clan leader. The clans probably were smaller in size than usual; altogether there were 62 clans. Members felt closely related, and clans were exogamous. One person was so much like another within the clan that members were like siblings to each other. If one was wronged, all others felt wronged and sought vengeance. In turn, if a clan member committed a wrong, vengeance could be taken on any clansman of the wrongdoer. At the clan level, politics were limited to marriage regulation, vengeance, and action for small-scale projects.

Each clan, however, was closely related to other clans, forming what is known as a *phratry*, that is, a grouping of two or more clans. Cibecue phratries were comprised of two to ten clans. They too were exogamous, and members were almost as closely linked as clan members. In another type of relation each clan had ties to other clans which were a more distant type of relation than among those in a phratry. In short, members of my clan were like my brothers and sisters; members in my phratry were almost as close as brothers and sisters. In still other clans, I had a "distant" but important link. As a result, if I were a capable individual I could go among any of the clans so related to me and raise a fighting or raiding party. Of course, in actuality, I would have to go among the widely scattered local groups to contact individuals. In most households I would be almost certain to find individuals either of my own clans, or my phratry, or a distantly related clan. All these people were obligated to support me; on the other hand, I had similar obligations toward them.

If these obligations seem overwhelming, recall that clan and phratry organizations regulate marriage. A man's father had to belong to a different clan and phratry; at marriage a wife and her relatives must belong to different clans and phratries. In this situation what are ego's relations like in regard to father and mother's brother? Will mother's brother exert all the authority, and will father be the warm affectionate figure typical of matrilineal organization?

The settlement patterns of Cibecue bring about variation. Mother's brother does wield authority over clan members, but as a man lives in a household and assumes more control, he exerts authority over his sons. Thus the Cibecue are useful to show the differences that can occur from the Hano model.

On the other hand, the Cibecue are more like other matrilineal peoples in relations between siblings and between a man and his parents-in-law. Brothers and sisters are committed to each other throughout life and exchange many mutual obligations. Actual contact, however, is limited and relations are marked by restraint. Similar behavior occurs when a man marries; he must show extreme respect for his mother-in-law. Indeed, most of the time they simply avoid each other. As a man proves himself, there is less restraint in the relation, but it is always marked by respect. Any deviation from this respect is cause for divorce, frequent among Apache for a number of other reasons as well.

Today, much of the former social organization prevails. Matriliny and clans are still important to the Cibecue Apache. Basso (1970:27) finds that only 21 clans now exist, and he notes that widely separated groups are known as "lines" with "branches" off the lines. With isolation a line becomes more and more differentiated from other formerly related lines. Population variation also affects lines or clans, and Basso predicts two clans will soon be extinct because they are now represented only by old men. Culture change has affected phratry organization even more dramatically. They are no longer exogamous and phratry obligations continually diminish. Further details of change in the social organization are aptly provided by individual cases.

As a case study Cibecue is valuable for showing how men going off to live in a matrilineage other than their own can exert some authority among those members. It is atypical for matriliny, yet the restriction of leadership to small-scale politics illustrates how males must exert authority over some matters within their household, while major politics may be handled differently. Further, the Cibecue illustrate some of the strain for men inherent in matriliny. A man is first a stranger in his home at marriage and must stay tied to his mother and her/his matrilineage. Over time this bond will weaken, and a man exerts authority among his wife's people. Still, the natal bond will never break for a man always remains tied to his sisters, their children, and his mother.

If patriliny were simply the opposite of matriliny, this dilemma of ties in two households would have to be faced by women where organization was by patrilineage. Yet a number of cases will show that the problem does not exist for women. On the other hand patrilineages still show a number of similarities to Hano and Cibecue matrilineages.

MAPUCHE, PATRILINY ON A RESERVATION

We begin our survey of patrilineal cases with Louis Faron's *Mapuche Indians of Chile*. Faron (1968:22) introduces Indian life as centering on kinship.

> The principal working relations of a day-to-day kind are those founded on blood ties. The Mapuche do not define blood ties in the manner of most Western peoples but conceive them in a framework of patrilineal descent.

The ancestral males who founded the different lineages are described in myth and legend; it is likely they did exist but doubtful that they all performed such noble deeds. Present lineages vary in size, averaging between two- and three-hundred. The lineages are generally localized; each Mapuche reservation is seen as being composed of one or two lineages.

The present organization is not too different from aboriginal times, but it is likely that the former lineages were smaller and occupied less territory. When reservations were established, lineages expanded in settling this new area. Pacification and new farming techniques contributed to population growth. The appointment of chiefs by the Chilean government altered political organization and to an extent affected the lineages. These "chiefs" were generally the elders of the dominant lineage on a reservation. Appointment gave a man more power than formerly; it also placed him over the small number of families on the reservation not in his lineage. This innovation probably meant politics operated on something other than kinship lines for the first time. However, the increase in size of the political unit was due mainly to growth in members of the lineage. This process spawned sublineages similar to the Cibecue "branchs." At some point, heads of these sublineages will become lineage founders, and new lineages will exist. Figure 4B illustrates this process. When the tie between the two original brothers is forgotten, two lineages will take the place of the original one.

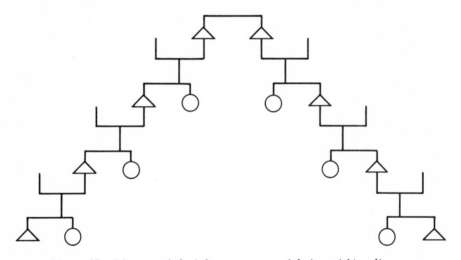

Figure 4B. Diagram of the inherent process of fission within a lineage.

Such splitting off seems inherent in the lineage organization described by Faron. He offers a taxonomy (1968:23–24) of the unilineal descent group.

1. *Maximal lineage*: all the agnatic descendants of an ancestor
2. *Lineage group*: the *living* members of the maximal lineage
3. *Localized lineage*: the members, both males and unmarried females, of a lineage group living together
4. *Minimal lineage*: a father and married sons, in effect an extended family
5. *Sublineages*: branches of the maximal lineage

In everyday life a Mapuche does not think of men around him as his lineage mates, but invariably when he needs help he turns to agnates. He helps or is helped by a brother, a father's brother, or a father's father's brother's son. The concept of lineage is not consciously dwelled upon, Faron (1968:24–25) says, "Yet the actions and thoughts of all adult males are rooted in the structure of patrilineality." Such action is in large part a result of patrilocality. Although the Indians seldom settle in the husband's father's household, they nearly always live on the husband's reservation. Also, they generally work their father's land or fields close to it. Obviously, agnates in day-to-day life are close to each other, have been reared together, and simply continue a well established pattern.

Occasionally, the ideals of agnatic cooperation cannot be met. Faron describes two brothers who worked their fields in common until their sons replaced them. After the death of one of the brothers, the surviving one added two more wives, which aroused complaints from his brother's son's wife. The nephew set up a new household nearby. Still, the split marked the beginning of a quarrel that eventually led to charges and countercharges of sorcery. Neither family liked to be reminded of the agnatic links that tied them, and two lineages will probably grow out of the factionalism. Possibly, one lineage will even move to another reservation.

Movement to another reservation sometimes occurs when a husband does not have access to land but his wife does. When the exceptional case of uxorilocal residence occurs, what effects on lineage membership would you predict for the husband and his children?

A Mapuche man in such a situation is considered unfortunate. Over time he begins to be slighted by his lineage, and his sons have great difficulty in validating their lineage rights. They are even more likely than their father to be unable to find land. Of course, like Maltese, Greeks, or the townsmen of San Pedro there is the alternative of city life, and many young men in such a position emigrate to Chilean farms, cities, or even service in the army. National life is certainly having its effects on Mapuche lineages, but even after years of contact patriliny remains a basic part of social organization.

YORUBA, PATRILINY WITHIN A KINGDOM

For a second example of patriliny we jump from South America to West Africa, where William Bascom (1969) describes in *The Yoruba of Southwestern Nigeria* the more than 10 million people of the Yoruba Kingdom organized around patrilineal principles. Interestingly, the Yoruba believe kinship ties should follow bilateral lines, and they recognize some ties of descent through females. However, patrilineal descent is institutionalized in the clan, and clan organization pervades Yoruba life. An individual is automatically a member of his father's clan and shares common names, facial marks, and taboos, as well as property rights, with a large number of relatives who are like siblings even when an exact tie cannot be traced. Male members tend to be especially close because of patrilocal residence. Where clans are too large, members must be scattered, and the localized lineages assume some of the aspects of the clan. The clan or lineage owns the compound where it dwells and also the outlying farm land. Religious and political titles likewise belong to clans. Such ownership retains property continuously since it is not held by individuals. As Bascom (1969:43) describes it, [the clan] is a self-perpetuating unit, as it includes the dead who may be reborn into the clan, as well as the living. Internally its members are stratified in terms of seniority, sex, and achieved status, but viewed from the outside the members of the same clan are social equivalents.

Within the clan, stratification usually follows seniority, for the head of a household is the eldest male in it. Within a compound the eldest male of the clan leads. In turn, each clan is headed by its senior male although, in the case of a lineage that has split off, its eldest male may have parallel authority with the clan elder. This clan elder is expected to settle disputes among clan members just as the household head is expected to maintain a peaceful household. Leaders have many other duties including administration of farm and household lands, sacrifices to prominent clan ancestors, ministration of medicine, and maintenance of physical structures.

The importance of seniority carries through to the various Yoruba kingdoms themselves. Yoruba-land, or western Nigeria, is occupied by about one-hundred kingdoms. Although political structures vary considerably, the Ile-Ife are fairly typical. Household compounds form the basis of this kingdom, a number of which are organized into precincts. Precincts are further organized into five wards, each headed by a *ward chief*. Particular clans are expected to furnish the leadership at each of these levels; the royal clan, largest in Ife, supplies the *king*. Ideally, the oldest male in the appropriate clan would be the leader, but the Yoruba realize high leadership demands high caliber. They readily pass over eligible candidates to secure capable leadership, although they do not go outside the eligible clans. Thus high leadership is inherited, but only along clan lines; sons do not necessarily inherit high leadership titles from their fathers.

Another type of leadership is reflected in the title of *palace chief*. Bascom (1969:33) explains how men of exceptional ability can achieve influence with the king and ward chiefs by first accumulating wealth and then using it in service to the king. Such individuals are usually thought of as belonging to the *Modewa* clan, which had a tradition of loyal aid, but any Ife man could join this clan if he could afford its expensive initiation. The West African kingdoms and other kinship states have generally devised solutions for passing over legitimate, but incapable, heirs in favor of able statesmen. But note that political organization continues to rest on principles of unilineal descent.

BUNYORO, THE TERMINOLOGY OF PATRILINY

In East Africa the political kingdom of the Nyoro, in their country of Bunyoro, rests on a contrasting basis. According to Beattie in *Bunyoro: An Africa Kingdom*, stratification results from a former conquest, and the king always comes from the conquering group known as the Bito. The Bito are supposedly like other Bunyoro clans, rather than a conquest group. Although all Bito have a common totem, only those who can demonstrate a real link to the founder (probably conqueror) have high prestige. To be considered for the kingship, the link must be especially close. Eligible descendants are actually princes, and they are expected to fight it out when the throne is vacated. In effect, a new king must kill many of his "brothers" to ascend the throne. Clearly, ability at political intrigue far overrides kinship links.

Still, patrilineal principles are important in the rest of Nyoro life. Although kinship seems to be diminishing in importance, it still governs much of a man's career. Like the Mapuche, the Nyoro in the past were strictly patrilocal so that localized groups were descent groups or their segments, but today exceptions to patrilocal residence are common. Clan membership gives a name and a totemic taboo and determines property and status rights. Clans also remain strictly exogamous.

Patriliny is clearly reflected in kinship terminology, and Beattie's (1960:49) description of it is most useful. Not all patrilineal societies have such a system of kinship terms, but many do. In fact, the one we are about to consider is known as the Omaha system, named after some Midwest Indians who serve as the prototype. The system is so different it may be confusing at first, but with your present under-standing of patriliny you could probably deduce it, for it is the logical outgrowth of a patrilineal organization. Simply remember that a person belongs to only one clan and has special links with fellow clansmen. He is tied to his mother's clan in a different way. He is an outsider there and sees its members as siblings. (Recall in Dozier's description of Hano that clansmen were like brothers and sisters when viewed by an outsider.)

For the Nyoro, a man calls his father and father's brother by the same term. The term may be glossed as "father," but more accurately it is a "male of my clan a generation above me." The term for father's sister is a feminine form of the term for father; Nyoro sometimes translate it as "female father." All the children of a father and father's brother are a man's "brothers" and "sisters." More accurately, they are "people of my clan in my generation." Will the children of father's sister be in this group? Of course not, because they will belong to their father's clan. Reciprocally, a man's sons and his brother's sons are in the patrilineage and in the category, "children of the clan"; sister's sons are in a different category because they belong to the clan of sister's husband. All clansmen, no matter how remote the actual genealogical links, fall into one of these three categories, glossed as father, sibling, child. Calling people by these terms implies duties and rights like those for close kin.

The tie to mother's clan is reflected likewise in terminology. A mother and her sister fall into the category "woman of the clan that mothered me." Mother's brother is thought of as a "male mother." Note that English speakers group mother's brother and father's brother in the same category as "uncle" and think of them as the same kind of relative. Beattie (1960:50) points out:

> To Nyoro, on the other hand, they are as different as can be, for one's father's brother is a member of one's own group, while a mother's brother is a member of an entirely different group. And a Nyoro's expectations and obligations in regard to members of these two distinct groups are quite different.

These basic relations are fundamental for an Omaha system. You might carry out the logic of the system further by considering how a man will be related to his mother's sister's children and his mother's brother's children. The key lies in whether these relatives can or cannot be in his clan. Which type of cousin can never be in his clan? Why? Schusky (1972) explores this terminology in depth in *Manual for Kinship Analysis*. It can be briefly illustrated in the following figure.

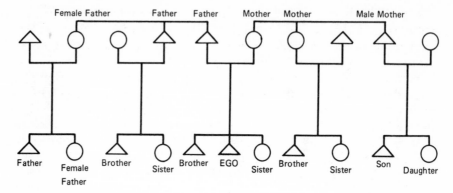

Figure 4C. English glosses for Nyoro terminology, an Omaha-type system.

KAPAUKU PAPUANS, PATRILINY WITH WARFARE AND SHIFTING AGRICULTURE

Let us leave Africa and go to the New Guinea Highlands for another example of patriliny. Here Leopold Pospisil (1963) offers us a case study, *The Kapauku Papuans of West New Guinea*, that shows considerable variation from the African forms. Some similar principles can still be found, however. (For a full discussion of African and New Guinea differences, see Barnes 1962.) The Kapauku Papuans were isolated from the modern world until studied by Pospisil, so they provide a case of patriliny uninfluenced by a major outside culture.

The Kapauku farm a high valley, growing root crops and raising pigs. Much of the soil is poor and fields must be fenced to keep out pigs. Agricultural work is hard and men engage in it full time as well as women. Clearing jungle is particularly arduous, but none of the farming tasks are easy. Farming is a full-time, year-round effort made more difficult by complexities of pig breeding and raising. When rare slack times do occur, men engage in pig trading, shelter and weapon manufacture, and warfare.

Much of social life centers on the pig trade, and men need to acquire pigs because they are necessary in ritual and in establishing prestige. The Kapauku go about acquiring pigs in the finest capitalistic tradition and spend their lives establishing or extending credit and building capital. In this operation a man aids and finds help among best friends and close maternal and paternal relatives. Indeed, in blood vengeance a man can count on any of his fourth cousins or any of his ancestors four generations removed.

In most other matters, however, patrilineal descent groups form the basis of operation. The Kapauku clan, or *tuma*, is a named, exogamous, totemic group. In legend, the Creator designated each of the clan ancestors to head the groups and declared that any marriages within a clan should be punished by death. In some cases two or more clans have a similar traditional link forming a phratry. The phratries share totems, and one is usually considered junior to the other; legend suggests it originated from the senior one. Unlike the clan, the phratries are not exogamous.

Phratry and clan do not function much beyond what has been described because members are widely scattered. Localized groups are made up of lineages or sub-lineages. Populations are small and members can trace accurately their genealogical agnates. If an individual settles in another village, it is usually temporary because important political and legal rights depend upon lineage membership. Within this group a headman maintains order and relations with other groups. The extra village contacts are necessary for defense and warfare because several villages are necessary to form loose political confederacies. The localized lineages or sublineages also have rights to land. Only a true lineage member can build a house and make a garden in the territory, or cut trees, trap, or collect plants in the steep, jungle areas connected to the territory.

Daily face-to-face contact, lifelong association, and mutual dependence make the lineage essential to the individual Kapauku. Pospisil (1963:39–40) phrases it thus:

> In their behavior members of the same sublineage exhibit mutual affection and a strong sense of belonging and unity. Any kind of friction within the group is regarded as deplorable, and it is the duty of the sublineage headman to settle peacefully the internal grievances as soon as possible. As a consequence of their close relationship, mutual support, and interest in each others' affairs, members of this group share a liability for each other's crimes against outsiders. The injured outside party often directs his self-redress indiscriminately against the property of any of the sublineage members. . . .

The localized lineage segment is much more dynamic than a large lineage or clan. Population fluctuates more quickly, agnatic links are forgotten sooner with sub-lineages splitting apart and settling elsewhere, smaller groups are annexed and absorbed in the process. Warfare can dramatically speed up these processes as virtually all males are wiped out or wide territories change hands. Of course, these processes must also work to change the large lineage and the clans, but their effects take much longer. In one generation the clan must appear to be a stable unit for its members.

Recall that the clan is not so important to the Kapauku as to the Yoruba, yet the lineage segment does embrace much of one's life. On the other hand, bilateral relations are of major importance on a number of occasions. A Kapauku's ties along these lines vary in nature and number from the Yoruba and even from the Nyoro, where the importance of the clan has diminished. One can only wonder if Mapuche clans did not closely resemble those of the Kapauku when warfare was significant to them. Unfortunately, the precontact data for Mapuche are unavailable.

ZINACANTECO, PATRILINY IN LOCALIZED GROUPS

We conclude our survey of patriliny with a case of Mayan Indians from Mexico. Evon Vogt (1970:32) provides another dynamic aspect of patriliny that must be considered a part of overall patrilineal organization. In *Zinacantecos of Mexico: A Modern Maya Way of Life*, he describes this aspect as the *developmental cycle*.

Before looking at the developmental cycle, a brief structural view of Zinacanteco, a Mayan *municipio*, is useful. Zinacantecos have localized patrilineages they call *sna*, which are shallow in depth, three or four generations in membership, and generally small. *Sna* members do not maintain connections with other agnates who settle elsewhere. The *sna* are much less significant than the Yoruba or Kapauku lineages, but members do live on adjacent lands inherited from ancestors. Also, the *sna* is headed by senior men with jural authority over many important matters, and some lineages own ritual paraphernalia essential for several yearly ceremonies.

The basic unit of the *sna* is what Vogt calls the *domestic group*. Given patrilocal residence and patrilineal inheritance, it could be described simply as a unit composed of fathers and their married sons. It is a patrilocal extended family very much like that of Vasilika with bilateral descent. Actual household arrangements vary only slightly from the Mediterranean village. A principal house is flanked by one or more houses occupied by the married sons. Only one "house cross," or shrine symbolic of a household, stands in the patio, and extended family membership centers upon it.

These domestic units vary considerably in composition, and much of the variation can be understood through analysis by developmental cycle. Such analysis allows a better understanding of how an insider views family life. Vogt tells us that any domestic group must contain males and females because men must grow corn and women must make tortillas. Commonly, a married couple provide such a basis, but other arrangements are possible. A widowed father may live with an unmarried daughter or even two sisters; a widow with an unmarried son may keep a household. Even in the course of "normal" events, households are seldom simply married couples.

We may start a cycle with the marriage of an eldest son. Courtship is expensive, and the son has no home of his own. He and his wife move in with his father. Mother-in-law and daughter-in-law friction and father's authority induce eventual movement to a new location. The second son then marries and will eventually move off; daughters leave when they marry. The youngest son will care for the parents in old age and will inherit the house and farm. When relations between a father and son are close, the new house may be built in the same compound. Even a man's son's sons may marry and live nearby, depending largely on the availability of land. If land is available, even a daughter may remain at home and have a husband settle with her. In short, conditions are much like those we examined in Greece and, to some extent, in Malta. In time the Zinacantecos might better be considered as having bilateral descent. Today, however, patrilineal descent groups are present and have important functions. They also affect the domestic group. Kinship terminology does not clearly reflect patriliny, but some neighboring Mayan villagers still have Omaha terminologies, and Vogt thinks Zinacantecos might once have had an Omaha system.

CHARACTERISTICS OF UNILINEAL DESCENT

Obviously, kinship terminologies are one aspect of unilineal descent groups. A Crow-type system, or the reverse of Omaha, is found almost always among matrilineal peoples; Omaha systems are common to patrilineal societies. The two systems have been described as mirror images of each other and have in common the categorizing together of relatives in different generations. They are said to "override" generation differences. What other generalizations can you make about unilineal descent systems? What is it that characterizes lineages or clans whether they are Hano, Yoruba, or Mapuche? You may form some generalizations only on the basis of one or two cases. Your generalizations can stand against a lack of evidence; they are only invalid if there is case material to prove they are wrong. At this point you should write out a number of generalizations based on the cases described here or other ethnographies you have read.

Meyer Fortes (1953) provided an early comprehensive list of unilineal descent group characteristics that showed clearly the large degree to which matrilineal organization resembled patrilineal organization. He noted first that unilineal groups are seldom, if ever, found among small societies with a rudimentary technology or little durable property. On the other hand, they are seldom found in societies where intensive specialization has led to large-scale occupational differentiations. When farm fields or herds are important, lineages often seem to be an answer to problems of property control. Recall, however, the Tibetan and Vasilikan cases as exceptions. In the control of property, the lineages become, in effect, a legal personality with corporate aspects. You may have expressed this notion in a variety of ways; it is the most striking quality of unilineal descent groups. As a legal person, the lineage is also a political person; it is responsible for internal control and external relations. The lineage must be structured so that it continues these functions despite the death of individual members; that is, the lineage continues in perpetuity. In the emphasis upon perpetuity a lineage may "cheat" in accounting for members. Descendants of a slave may be made lineage mates if their descendants are necessary to continue a lineage. Often children of a female member are made members of a patrilineage if they are needed. Recall the Hano solution. Members of Hopi and even Navajo clans with the same names as Hano clans were included to insure perpetuity.

Not only is the link to descendants essential, but lineages invariably look to their ancestors as well. A founding ancestor cements together his living descendants. Frequently associated with the ancestor is some totem, totemic taboos, and a legend that accounts for the "closeness" of lineage or clan members. Recall that for the Kapauku, the Creator himself designated the original clan leaders, and among the Yoruba a major duty of the clan elder was to sacrifice to the ancestors and venerate their spirits. Further, recall the Hano Bear who spoke of his lineage in terms of his mother's mother's mother, and how he immediately balanced the line with his sister's daughter's daughter's children.

Relations with the unilineal descent group became so close because of common ancestry that clansmen are like siblings. A Hano Bear recognized even a Navajo Bear as a "brother." Apache were explicit in noting other clansmen as brothers or sisters, and Nyoro kinship terminology reflects the closeness of clan relations. The kinship terms applied to fellow clansmen are never extended to kinsmen of a different clan or lineage. Rules of vengeance further reflect the closeness of relations. If a Kapauku wrongs me, I can seek vengeance on any of his clansmen. In turn,

I am obligated to help redress wrongs against any member of my lineage if I am a Cibecue Apache. Indeed, almost all lineages have similar vengeance rules not only because of close kinship but also because the lineage has a jural personality.

In order for the descent group to act as one, authority has to be clear-cut. Recall how often leadership positions were integral parts of lineages and clans. Among Yoruba, a man clearly headed a household, another leader headed the localized sub-lineage, another man led the lineage, and another elder headed the clan. Even where ability was much needed and recognized as vital, as in the kingship, descent principles were operative. The king had to come from the royal clan, and he was recognized as the leader of that clan even if he had to kill some elders to reach that position.

The clear-cut authority patterns within descent groups make internal control possible and strengthen group ties. Yet such a structure also allows fission, a process seemingly inevitable among unilineal descent groups. Sublineage heads may lead members astray, and a new lineage arises; recall the Mapuche case of two brothers whose sons finally split apart. The Kapauku provide the best illustration of how warfare and population changes bring fairly rapid fission to their lineages and clans. The fission process among the Zinacantecos operates to make a residence group resemble a bilateral extended family. Conversely, the cases provide examples of fusion. Mapuche men who move onto a new reservation may be absorbed by the resident lineage; it is even more likely that their children or grandchildren will be. Victorious Kapauku often incorporated their enemies into their lineages, at least women and children.

If you were able to make half the generalizations included here, you did very well. Anthropologists had accumulated far more cases of unilineal descent before they came to realize the many similarities between patriliny and matriliny. For a full discussion of unilineal descent group structure consult Fortes' (1953) article "The Structure of Unilineal Descent Groups." Significant differences, however, do exist between the two forms: In patriliny the line of authority and line of descent are in the same link, whereas the line of authority in matriliny follows males and descent links are through females. What does this difference mean in terms of structural differences? How will it affect relations between males and females or sex-linked statuses such as husband or wife? Again, write out some generalizations about how patrilineal descent groups may vary from matrilineal descent groups before reading further.

Schneider and Gough (1962:1–32) provide half-a-dozen generalizations pointing up the differences. Basically, Schneider notes that matrilineal groups must retain control over both male and female members, while patrilineal groups easily give up the females. The overt control and power that resides in men require that male members remain close enough to sisters to continue their descent group activities. For Hano Indians the problem is minimal because villagers live in compact settlements. A man is never far from his mother and sisters even when he resides with his wife. Residence is more of a problem with Cibecue Apache, however, and young men find it difficult to return to their lineage. Enough of them do return to maintain lineage activity, but note that elder men gradually shift their authority to their wife's household. This authority is limited to the household and some economic matters, however, and power within the lineage must be exercised by its members.

The strain between a man's commitment to his lineage and to his wife's domicile is matched by another inherent strain in matriliny. A man must be interested in his sister's reproduction because she perpetuates his own lineage, yet she is a tabooed sex object. It is probable that matrilineal societies are the most likely to exaggerate brother and sister avoidance in order to solve the problem. Another solution is to claim ignorance of sex as a factor in reproduction, as do a number of South Seas islanders, who refuse to acknowledge any correlation. The Tiwi will illustrate this belief in the next chapter.

Such a claim does not eliminate fatherhood, but it certainly changes the nature of the status. Indeed, the father/husband status is not essential for matriliny—witness the Nayar; although it is customary, the behavior of fatherhood is much different. Rarely does he exert much authority over his own children; instead he directs what we think of as fatherlike behavior toward his sister's children.

All of these factors lead to a conclusion that strong ties between a husband and wife are incompatible with matrilineal descent groups. Recall the case of Apache divorce. Although Hano marriages are fairly stable, Dozier notes they are exceptional among matrilineal Pueblos; even so their divorce rate is high. Men simply cannot get deeply attached to their wife's matrilineage because they remain tied elsewhere. On the other hand, women are sometimes nearly assimilated in their husband's patrilineage, for it is not their ties to any lineage that are of any major importance but, rather, their ties to husband and children that are fundamental.

These rather obvious generalizations are offered as an introduction to unilineal descent groups. Further analysis can be found in Schneider and Gough (1962). You should be well prepared now for the level of theoretical work that appears in this volume and in professional journals.

One final aspect of kinship theory will be introduced in the next chapter. Up to now we have looked at kinship largely in terms of descent and have examined behavior and structure among consanguineal links. Marriage has been mentioned only in passing. Yet marriage serves to ally kinship units such as descent groups, combining them to provide a basic, wide-ranging net of kinship that is fundamental to society.

EXERCISES

1. In matrilineal groups in-marrying males have special problems with respect to each other. For instance, if I were a Huron male, I would be in a longhouse with my wife. The men married to her mother and sisters could all be from different lineages. Then not only would my wife's brothers be "strangers," but my brothers-in-law would also be of strange or different lineages. As "outsiders" we should share something in common, but if our lineages differ we can only be suspicious of each other. What could guarantee that the brothers-in-law and even the father-in-law would share the same lineage membership?

2. In the diagram below check off which persons would constitute in Hano the typical Tewa household of Ego. Then note which ones belong to the lineage of Ego.

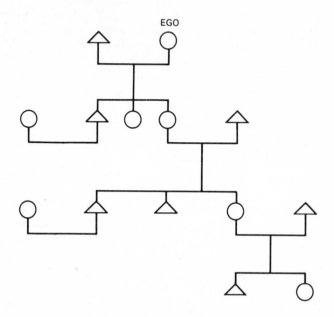

SUGGESTED READINGS FROM THE CASE STUDIES

Edward Dozier, *The Pueblo Indians of North America.* In Part III Dozier provides
    a comparison of Eastern and Western Pueblo kinship systems, which admirably
    introduces the method of crosscultural comparison. Although all his hypotheses
    may still not be "proven," the case indicates quite well the nature of anthropo-
    logical problems and their investigation.

OTHER READINGS

David Schneider and Kathleen Gough (eds.), *Matrilineal Kinship.* This collection
    of matrilineal cases is useful as an extension of the survey of matriliny, but
    it is even more useful as illustration of how anthropologists may generalize
    from their data.

5

Descent and Affinity

A neat solution to Exercise 1 of Chapter 4 can be obtained by simple marriage rules. All in-marrying males who are residing matrilocally with their wives and in-laws will be united if society is divided into two exogamous groups. Such a dual organization is so common that anthropologists designate the groups with the special term *moiety*. If my wife is a member of moiety *A*, her sisters will also be *A*. I must be a *B* to marry her; so also must all the men married to her sisters. In a sense they will all be my brothers, at least moiety brothers. Moiety or dual organization works equally well with patriliny, and it is widespread among both matrilineal and patrilineal societies.

When societies are organized into exogamic moieties with unilineal descent, "cousins" become a totally different kind of relative. A translation of "cousin" is virtually impossible. To appreciate the difference, assume you are in a patrilineal moiety known as the red moiety. You, your father, and his brother and sister are reds. Your mother, her sister and brother are members of the white moiety. Each of these individuals must marry a member of the opposite moiety; the children of such unions will belong to the moiety of their father. What will be the moiety membership of your father's brother's children and your mother's sister's children?

Your father's brother is a red so his children are red, like yourself. Your mother's sister is a white; she must marry a red; therefore, her childen will be red. But what about father's sister's children and mother's brother's children? These "cousins" will be white members. Before going farther, be sure you understand why these differences occur. A diagram may help; the shaded symbols in Figure 5A are members of the red moiety.

Since your mother's sister's children and father's brother's children (recall the technical term for them is *parallel cousins*) are in the same moiety as you, they are much like a brother and sister. Often in terminology these parallel cousins are equated with siblings. However, father's sister's children and mother's brother's children (known technically as *cross cousins*) are in the opposite moiety. They are in a quite different category. Indeed, they are in the marriageable moiety and generally are potential spouses. In some societies the cross cousins are the only eligible spouses, and the topic of cross-cousin marriage has been a major one in anthropology.

Anthropologists, however, exaggerated the importance and widespread distribution of cross-cousin marriage because it was so easy to confuse the practice with

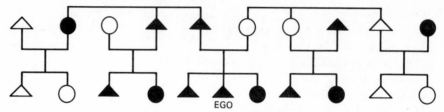

Figure 5A. Membership differences in patrilineal moiety organization.

simply moiety exogamy. That is, a potential wife is anyone in the opposite moiety. I may have a term for all those women that could be translated "potential wife." I also might use this word as a kinship term for my female cross cousins as well, and I might likely marry one of them. There is no easy way to distinguish between cross-cousin marriage and moiety exogamy because kinship terms generally are difficult to translate. Anthropologists are attempting to achieve greater accuracy in interpreting kinship terms through a method known as *componential analysis.* The method is well introduced by Paul Turner (1972:26–29) in *The Highland Chontal,* which illustrates the procedure with both English and Chontal terminology. Although componential analysis may clarify the meanings of terminological systems, it will remain difficult to determine exactly all the factors that influence marriage choice because many exceptions occur regardless of rules.

TIWI, CONTROLLING WOMEN IN MARRIAGE ALLIANCES

Let us look at a particular case to understand the problem better. C. W. M. Hart and Arnold Pilling give us *The Tiwi of North Australia,* a case study that examines (1960:27) the classical system of cross-cousin marriage known as the *Kariera type.* The Kariera were an Australian aborigine community organized into patrimoieties. In day-to-day life bands were made up of small numbers of agnates, who gave sisters to other bands of the opposite moiety in exchange for wives. A further organization rule divided and categorized people by generation so that people of alternate generations fell into the same category. Simply put, a man and his father's father and his son's son were in the same generation grouping. The two moieties and the two generation groupings made four sections that regulated marriage, and exchanges had to be between moieties and within the generation grouping. Essentially, the system is simple, but anthropologists have complicated too often their explanations of it. Fortunately Robin Fox (1967:175–191) provides a clear explanation for those interested in pursuing the subject.

This Kariera type of organization is the foundation for Tiwi practices described by Hart and Pilling, but they note that, alone, it could not accomodate all the complexities added by the Tiwi. The notable additions are practices known as infant bestowal and widow remarriage. These practices are valuable for illustrating both marriage as alliance and the structural effects of regularized marriage exchanges.

The Tiwi are exceptional in a number of ways, yet their elaboration of the exchange of women is simply the epitomy of what many peoples do. For instance, many peoples practice *sister exchange.* In effect, I say to you: "I will give you my sister in marriage if you will give me your sister." Only the Tiwi have control over other women besides their sisters, and there has been a peculiar development: Tiwi men control some women who are not of their lineage or clan. For example, the Tiwi are matrilineal, but a man controls his daughter. Actually, as Hart and Pilling emphasize, it is the husband of the pregnant woman who controls the marriage of his wife's female babies. (Since the Tiwi deny any connection between sexual intercourse and conception, "fatherhood" is not a useful concept. Recall from Chapter 4 why matrilineal societies tend to deny a relation between sex and conception.)

A man exercises his control immediately, and the female baby is married at birth. Likewise, a widow is remarried at the death of her husband. Whereas most people believe all females *should* be married, the Tiwi insist that all females *must* be married. What consequences follow from these rules? An obvious one is that no Tiwi are illegitimate. But, if the numbers of males and females are about equal and young males are unmarried, who will the "excess" females marry? Clearly the Tiwi must be polygynous, and the rate of plural marriage is high.

Hart and Pilling (1960:15) emphasize that men exercise their rights of bestowal because they expect a tangible return. "Put bluntly, in Tiwi culture daughters were an asset to their father, and he invested these assets in his own welfare." The daughters went to a friend and ally or someone a man wanted as an ally. Thus the recipient was usually a man of nearly equal age, hence thirty to forty years older than the newly born baby; in return, the bestower could expect to receive a wife from his ally. In effect, infant daughters were exchanged instead of sisters. Another type of "investment" was to select a much younger son-in-law who would care for a man in his old age. Such a youth would have to "show promise" as a hunter and fighter. Once a wife was bestowed upon him, he looked even better as an investment, and other men started bestowing upon him. The more wives such a youth acquired, the more prestige he had; he could expect some help from all his fathers-in-law, but he also might be overwhelmed with responsibilities. As you might imagine, the process entangled men in a host of obligations, and bestowal of a wife's daughter was a complicated process. The practice (1960:16) caught men ". . . in an intricate network of previous commitments, residual interests, and contingent promises made by other men."

At the earliest, a man married at the age of twenty-five. Since his wife did not join him until she was fifteen or more, a man was forty, usually much older, before he began living with a wife. Naturally, the average Tiwi woman became a widow, but even as an adult some man had control over her marriage rights. Generally, when men above her in generation passed away, her brothers or own sons gained control. Often a widow was married to the brother of her dead husband (a common practice known as the *levirate*), but other claims could prevail. Only a small percentage of marriages reflected the levirate custom. The *sororate* also occurred: In effect, a man bestowed two or more of his daughters on the some man. Such bestowal reflected a desire to cement a relationship with another man.

The authors (1960:26) summarize these practices in explicit terms of alliance.

The aim of bestowal was to win friends and influence people, and a bestowal of a child who died before she reached the son-in-law did a father little good. A shrewd father could avoid this risk by following the sororate principle; a stupid or feckless father who scattered his daughters widely could well end up with as many disappointed sons-in-law as friendly ones, as the infantile and child mortality took its heavy toll of his young daughters.

You will see from this excerpt why a *pattern* of bestowal could develop. Another interpretation is that women began to move along regular lines. A man consistently bestowed women on another man or his brothers. Once an alliance was created by one marriage, it was reinforced by further marriages. Now revive the initial question of this chapter. How might a person take consanguine relatives with him when he locates among a spouse and her consanguines?

Among Tiwi a woman is likely to be accompanied by sisters as co-wives or as wives married to her husband's brothers. In the case of the Huron, a man's brothers or other lineage mates may regularly marry into his wife's lineage. Two points should emerge from this discussion. The first is that marriage serves as alliance between men, who, after all, wield power; women simply serve as part of the contract. However, women are not considered merely chattel in the process, and they are not equated with other forms of goods or property. Once alliances are created, men are generaly wise to protect their investment by "investing" further; that is, they bestow more women on their sons-in-law or the group that first received women from them. The second major point is that giving a wife indebts the recipient, who will often reciprocate with service, food, or other property (mistakenly interpreted as a bride price), although such goods or service never fully equate with women or their reproductive power. Bride-takers remain subordinate to wife-givers, and this fact of life makes marriage a political affair, for most political systems must be understood in terms of kinship and marriage. Edmund Leach (1954) provides a classic example. Of course, men may simply reciprocate in exchanging women and remain equals. Or dual organizations, such as moieties, may reciprocate directly because of an exogamous rule. However, where multiple groups exist, as in the case of clans, direct reciprocity is less likely, and if women start "moving" consistently from one group to another, the recipients become indebted and subordinate to the donor groups.

In the case of the Tiwi we see both these principles in operation. The Tiwi in theory believed that a man should bestow his daughter on his sister's son. What happens in regard to clan affiliation in such a case?

I have control over my daughter although she is a member of my wife's clan (remember the Tiwi are matrilineal). My sister's son is the closest male to me in my clan. What could be better than marrying my daughter to my clan heir? Nothing, unless I could find a better man than my nephew. Since Tiwi looked hard for such a son-in-law, they often found rationalizations for frequently deviating from the norm. But reconsider the ideal relationship from a groom's point of view. For a man, his mother's brother arranged a marriage for him with his daughter. As a Tiwi I expect to marry my mother's brother's daughter unless, of course, uncle finds a better prospect. If my uncle had married his mother's brother's daughter, as expected, then I would marry into the same clan he did. In effect, my mother's brother would be my father-in-law just as my sister's son would be my son-in-law. In such a case women move regularly from one clan to another and in-marrying spouses find themselves accompanied by clan or lineage mates. But if one lineage regularly takes women without reciprocating, it will become subordinate to the other. Of course, it gives its women in the same way to another lineage that, in turn, becomes subordinate to it. In theory A gives to B, B gives to C, and C gives to A. Overall, the society is neatly balanced, but any one lineage stands as subordinate and superordinate to another. The exchange can be diagramed as follows.

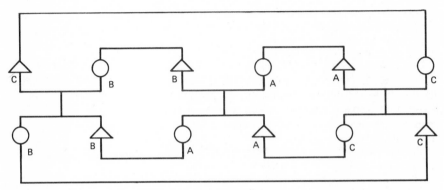

Figure 5B. Indirect alliance through matrilateral cross-cousin marriage.

BUNYORO, GOPALPUR, AND MAPUCHE: INDIRECT EXCHANGE IN MARRIAGE ALLIANCE

These marriage practices are so different from what we think of as our own that you are likely skeptical or suspect. You think the Tiwi are simply an odd, esoteric community. Therefore, let us quickly sample some other cases. You are already familiar with Bunyoro, an African kingdom far removed from Australia. Let us look at what Beattie (1960:56) has to say of Nyoro marriage. In some cases, "A man might say to a close friend: 'My wife is pregnant; I give her child to you!' He would mean by this that if his child were a girl his friend could have her as a wife for his son." How like the Tiwi! Further, Beattie notes the practice shows that

> traditionally the woman is not one of the two contracting parties in marriage; she is rather the subject of a transaction between two men and the groups of kin they belong to. Secondly, it stresses the fact that for Nyoro the woman's group is always the giver and the husband the receiver. And the giver always has superior status, while the receiver is subordinate and must be humble and respectful to his prospective in-laws.

In his own household a Nyoro does not have such feelings for his wife, who is clearly an inferior to her husband. She kneels in handing him his food and addresses him as "sir," but she has rights to food, clothing, and fields. If abused, she can turn to her kin, who are able to exert authority because of their son-in-law's submission.

As a result of this subordination, a Nyoro always feels constraint in relations with his wife's people. They are "those who make us feel ashamed"; that is, if a man behaved overfamiliarly with them, he would be ashamed. Beattie (1960:58) tells us that a man's feelings toward in-laws are highly ambivalent: "On the one hand he feels gratitude and respect toward them, for they have given him a wife; on the other hand he is conscious of fear and even hostility toward them, for they are not his own people, but outsiders."

Let us again jump continents to India to continue our sample. In the south Indian village of Gopalpur, Alan Beals (1962:24) reports a play enacted annually that illustrates a myth emphasizing the importance of marriage as alliance. The two most important themes of social life stand out: (1) cooperation within the village that is secured through lineage and neighborhood ties, and (2) cooperation among different villages that is achieved through marriage.

In contrast to Tiwi these Indians are patrilineal, and their beliefs of conception are a near opposite. Whereas Tiwi regarded sperm as unimportant, the villagers of Gopalpur see sperm as the seed and woman as the mere soil for planting. All agnates contain the same seed and are brothers and sisters; a bride and groom must always be of different seed or different lines of descent.

In looking for a bride a man can be certain that his mother is of a different seed from himself and his father. Likewise, his mother's brother will be of a different seed. Therefore, his mother's brother's daughter is a prospective bride. Similarly, his sister must marry someone of a different seed, and her children will be of their father's seed, necessarily different from his own. Thus marriage with a sister's daughter is also possible, and Gopalpur villagers see it as desirable. Structurally anthropologists know that recurrent sister's daughter marriage would simply be another form of mother's brother's daughter marriage. How can this be? Since you have been introduced to kinship diagrams, use some charts to understand the equation.

If you cannot chart it, imagine the following. If you are expected to marry your sister's daughter, then your maternal uncle is expected to marry his sister's daughter. His sister's daughter is your sister. If he is married to your sister, then your sister's daughter is also your mother's brother's daughter. Mull it over or try to chart it again.

The reasoning of villagers about conception is more likely a rationalization of mother's brother's daughter marriage rather than a cause of it. Anthropologists are not certain of the cause either, but the practice does result in clearcut standings between lineages. One lineage regularly receives women from another lineage, while its own women are given elsewhere. As a result lineages have clear subordinate–superordinate relations with each other. Beals (1962:27)* describes the effects vividly:

> When, at the age of thirteen or fourteen, Ego observes the appearance of a stranger of middle age wearing a yellow silk turban and carrying a staff, he greets him, "What 'mother's brother,' why have you come?" If the stranger does not look wealthy and well dressed, Ego might well address him as "father," "older brother," or "grandfather." All of these latter terms imply a certain familiarity,

* From Alan Beals, *Gopalpur: A South Indian Village*, Holt, Rinehart and Winston, Inc., 1962. By permission of the publisher.

even a kind of equality; Ego certainly does not want to suggest to this man in the impressive yellow silk turban that Ego considers him to be no better than his own father. The "mother's brother" is unquestionably superior to Ego's father, for it is the "mother's brother" who "gave" Ego's mother to Ego's father. The "mother's brother" is invariably treated with honor and deference when he visits the village; hence, a superior stranger is a "mother's brother." Although a "mother's brother" might conceivably be in fact a brother of Ego's mother, he may also be the man who married Ego's father's sister or Ego's older sister. In any case, the "mother's brother" is an older man, married to an older woman, and belonging to Line II [a lineage superior to Ego]. If the "mother's brother" has a daughter, that daughter may well become Ego's bride. In fact, Ego cannot marry any girl unless her father has been identified as a "mother's brother" or a "younger sister's husband." To people in Gopalpur, "mother's brother" means primarily "giver of the bride."

If the stranger is himself looking for a bride, or means to ask some favor of Ego, he may, in turn, address Ego as "mother's brother." If the stranger wishes to indicate that he considers himself to be a perfect equal to Ego, he may address him as "brother-in-law" meaning "younger sister's husband." If the stranger wishes to express his superiority to Ego, he addresses him as "sister's son" which also means "receiver of the bride" or "daughter's husband." Except for the term "younger sister's husband," which is rarely used and is considered rude or humorous, all men in Line II are divided into "Bridegivers," older men married to older women, and "Bridetakers," younger men married to younger women.

We can summarize briefly some salient points about marriage. The exchange of women among most communities is for the purpose of creating alliances. Although Westerners are familiar with royal families arranging marriages for such purposes, they are usually unaware of how common the practice is in other cultures for virtually all marriages. Secondly, when a man or his group gives a woman in marriage, the recipient and his group reciprocate with property or service, but such a return never quite matches the value of women, because it seems their reproductive power is judged of unredeemable worth. If the recipient is able to return women to the group that gave him his bride, then relations can remain fairly equal. However, it often happens that groups begin giving women in one direction while receiving them from another. In such a case bridegivers invariably become superior to bridetakers. The phenomenon has been well illustrated for Bunyoro and Gopalpur; we can also quickly add the Mapuche to show examples from three different continents.

Recall the patrilineal Mapuche of Chile who reside patrilocally. Faron (1968: 43–44) states that Mapuche never marry women of their own lineage by definition, nor do they marry any woman related to their sisters by marriage. Yet they do prefer to marry a relative, and they make such marriages almost without exception. They accomplish this goal in the same way Gopalpur villages find women of a "different seed." Faron shows how it is accomplished.

These lineages . . . do not intermarry in a haphazard fashion. Rather, men from lineage *x* marry women from lineage *y* but give their daughters in marriage to men of lineage *z*, never to men from lineage *y*, which would constitute incest. This is merely another way of stating . . . [that] a man can marry a woman connected to him on his mother's side of the family but is forbidden to marry a woman connected to him through marriage of his lineage sister. In genealogical terms, this may be stated as follows: a man can marry a woman in the category of "mother's brother's daughter" but is forbidden to marry a woman in the category of "father's sister's daughter."

It is difficult for students to accept the fact of a definite preference for mother's brother's daughter among many different peoples. Why is that one type of "cousin" singled out? In the first place the girl is not a "cousin" except in our terms. Secondly, she is not exactly a mother's brother's daughter either (at least it is not as important as anthropologists sometimes try to make it). Faron's (1968:44) interpretation is illuminating.

> The Mapuche pay much less attention to genealogical ramifications than the anthropologist does, and it is misleading to phrase their notions of a perfect marriage in genealogical terms. Rather, the Mapuche have to know only one thing in order to contract proper marriage: The girl he calls ñuke is the ideal marriage partner.

In other words society is so well organized that individuals have little trouble in operating within it. It is anthropologists who have difficulty in formulating the structure of the society, and social scientists who have even more difficulty in determining why the structure should come into existence in the first place. The reasons for matrilateral cross-cousin marriage remain obtuse, although the subject was probably the most important issue in social anthropology during the last two decades.

Dual organization with direct reciprocity, however, is a far more common structure for society, and introductory students should first master the features of such forms. Fortunately, the Yanomamö provide an excellent example, and their ethnographer, Napoleon Chagnon, provides a survey of relevant theory as well as description.

YĄNOMAMÖ, THE DIRECT EXCHANGE OF EXOGAMOUS MOIETIES

Chagnon's book *Yąnomamö: The Fierce People* (1968) is so valuable that I will not attempt to summarize it as I have done with others. He vividly describes the remarkable adjustments this people has made to the tropical rain forest of Venezuela in Chapter 2, the even greater difficulties they encounter in warfare, and their attempts to protect themselves through alliances. As you should expect, marriages are an integral feature of the alliances created, and the exchanges of women continually enter into negotiations. A fierce emphasis upon equality and individuality immediately suggests that most exchanges of women will be reciprocal, and Yąnomamö marriage is described as bilateral cross-cousin marriage. We say that in bilateral cross-cousin marriage a man may marry either his mother's brother's daughter or his father's sister's daughter. The brothers of these women receive my sisters in return. Actually, a model of such marriage shows that a regular practice of such marriage will make my mother's brother's daughter and my father's sister's daughter one and the same person! Before you say "impossible" recall how mother's brother's daughter and sister's daughter so easily became one and the same. This time, think what would happen if your father would have said to a man, "I will give you my sister in marriage if you give me your sister." Your father's sister would be your mother's brother's wife. Therefore, your father's sister's daughter would also be your mother's brother's daughter. In effect, one group is simply exchanging women with another group. In my group everyone in my generation is essentially my brother and sister; everyone in the opposite group is my potential wife and brother-in-law. The wives and brothers-in-law are also my cross cousins. Whether I am marrying a "potential wife" or a "cross cousin" is largely a semantic problem created by previous anthropologists. The structure of the situation again can be clarified by a diagram. You might compare Figure 5C below with Figure 5A; it is essentially the same, except parallel cousins are eliminated and the cross cousins rearranged.

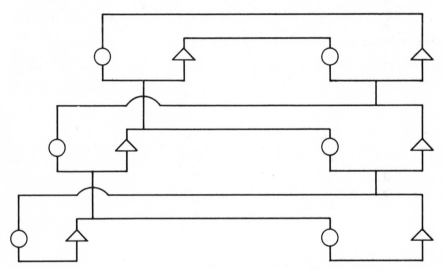

Figure 5C. Bilateral cross-cousin marriage over three generations.

Other problems do exist, however, and I have oversimplified some of those treated here. An excellent further introduction is available in Chapter 3 of *Yąnomamö*. You should be well prepared now to analyze ten genealogies documented by Chagnon, who surveys marriage practices within the dual organization of Yąnomamö. He further provides a brief survey of a controversy in British anthropology about the relative importance of descent ties and marriage ties. For a further examination of this controversy and other concerns in social anthropology you may turn to an intriguing title "Some Muddles in the Models: Or, How the System Really Works" by David Schneider (1965).

Without doubt the theories about kinship are the most sophisticated ones in social anthropology and possibly all of anthropology and sociology. Some of the topics with which the theories are concerned are of minor importance. For example, very few societies today practice unilateral cross-cousin marriage. Yet such an esoteric practice has given us a better understanding of the nature of society and the nature of norms. Social scientists are still far from understanding how norms originate, but the question is as basic to social science as the origin of species was

to biology. Many of us in anthropology are betting that we will eventually determine the origin of norms from the study of kinship, but as this introduction to the
subject should indicate, we still have some distance to go.

EXERCISE

1. Diagram matrilateral cross-cousin marriage over four generations. Diagram
5B will start you. Then diagram patrilateral cross-cousin marriage for four generations. Compare the two diagrams carefully. What is the difference between the two
practices? Hint: What is different about the exchange of women in the two
systems?

SUGGESTED READINGS FROM THE CASE STUDIES

Napoleon Chagnon, *Yąnomamö: The Fierce People.* The first two chapters are
    worth reading as an introduction to Chapter 3. The third chapter cannot be
    read lightly, but if you have read this unit carefully, you are prepared to
    appreciate fully marriage and descent principles as they function among a
    particular people (incidentally a most intriguing group of people and one
    very well described by Chagnon).

Glossary

Affinity: A kinship tie created by marriage. Affinal ties are contractual and can be broken in contrast to the enduring ties of consanguinity.

Agnatic descent: A system that traces descent through males. The term is intended to be more precise than patrilineal descent; it is meant to emphasize descent through males rather than "the father."

Avunculocal residence: A norm that requires a newly married couple to live with or near the groom's mother's brother. In such residence, a man usually will inherit statuses from his mother's brother. If he has married his matrilateral cross cousin, avunculocal residence is, in effect, matrilocal residence. *See also* Matrilocal residence, Neolocal residence, and Patrilocal residence.

Bilateral cross-cousin marriage: An institution by which a man is expected to marry either his mother's brother's daughter or his father's sister's daughter. Where all marriages are in this fashion, these two relations will be the same person. *See also* Unilateral cross-cousin marriage.

Bilateral descent: A system that traces descent through both males and females. Since ancestors and descendants increase at a geometric ratio, bilateral descent cannot be a basis for descent groups unless limited by generation or to particular ancestors or descendants. Bilateral descent is the practice of most Westerners who do not form descent groups, nor do they remember all their ancestors through many generations. *See also* Cognatic descent.

Bride wealth: Goods or service given to the wife's group at her marriage. The wealth exchange at marriage is multifunctional and complex. It is far more than a simple "price" for the bride. Bride wealth is a substitute term for "bride price" to indicate this complexity. *See also* Progeny price.

Clan: Two or more lineages united by a putative ancestor. The ancestor is usually a superhuman figure or totem assumed to be a common ancestor of all clan members. Since lineages are determined by descent through one sex, clans also are either matrilineal or patrilineal.

Cognatic descent: A system that traces descent through either sex. In practice, cognatic descent groups are usually agnatic; a people may maintain that descent is through males, but, in practice, they frequently incorporate a female link in tracing ascent. *See also* Bilateral descent and Unilineal descent.

Consanguinity: A kinship tie based on "blood" or through one that can be traced through descent. The father's brother is a consanguine relative who may be described as a father's father's son. *See also* Affinity.

Corporate group: A group that exists in perpetuity. Kinship groups like lineages and clans are structured to be corporate; the nuclear family or kindred, because of their structure, cannot be corporate. Enduring political, economic, and religious functions must be invested in corporate groups generally.

Cross cousins: Children of one's mother's brother or father's sister. Children of siblings of opposite sex are cross cousins.

Endogamy: A rule or norm that requires marriage within some particular group. Ethnic or religious groups are often endogamous as are castes.

Exogamy: A rule or norm that requires marriage outside some particular group. The norm is sometimes confused with an incest rule. For instance, the American family is not exogamous; it is an incest rule that requires members to seek mates elsewhere. Lineages and clans are almost always exogamous.

Extended family: A unit composed of parents, their children, and an addition of kin. A nuclear family may be extended by additional spouses, by one or more of the parents or siblings of the parents, or by any other kin. In many societies most families cycle through nuclear and extended stages. *See also* Nuclear family.

Incest: Sexual relations between close kin. Incest rules forbid such relations; indirectly, the rules thus regulate marriage. Exogamy and endogamy rules about marriage, however, should be kept distinct from incest rules (norms about sex).

Kindred: The close kin of Ego. Parents, their siblings, and all their children comprise the kindred. Only Ego and his siblings share the same kindred; thus this kin group is never corporate; its functions will center on Ego, as in times of life crises.

Lineage: A line of relatives that traces ascent and descent through one sex or the other. A female line is a matrilineage; a male line is a patrilineage. *See also* Matrilineal descent and Patrilineal descent.

Matrilineal kin: Relatives on the mother's side; those to whom one can trace a tie starting with mother.

Matrilineal descent: A system that traces descent through females. A man inherits group membership through his mother, but it is better to understand the descent group as formed on a line of females. Thus a man traces his ascent through his mother; equally important is descent through his sister.

Matrilocal residence: A norm that requires a newly married couple to reside with or near the wife's kin, usually her mother's group. *See also* Avunculocal residence, Neolocal residence, and Patrilocal residence.

Moiety: One of two divisions in a society. Such dual organizations are usually exogamous. Exogamous moieties with unilineal descent form well-structured groups with regular marriage practices.

Neolocal residence: A norm that requires a newly married couple to establish an independent residence. The practice is comparatively rare. *See also* Avunculocal residence, Matrilocal residence, and Patrilocal residence.

Network: Both kin and non-kin statuses to whom Ego has rights and responsibilities. The network is the result of choice, yet the choosing is highly structured by kin ties.

Nuclear family: The family of parents and children. Two spouses and a child or children comprise the nuclear family. *See also* Extended family.

Parallel cousins: Children of one's mother's sister or father's brother. Children of siblings of the same sex are parallel cousins.

Patrilateral kin: Relatives on the father's side; those to whom one can trace a link starting with father.

Patrilineal descent: A system that traces descent through males. A man inherits group membership through his father, although it is better understood as descent traced through males. Thus a man's sister is in his descent group, but not her children. His own children and his brother's children will be in the patrilineage. *See also* Agnatic descent.

Patrilocal residence: A norm that requires a newly married couple to reside with or near the husband's kin, usually his father's group. *See also* Avunculocal residence, Matrilocal residence, and Neolocal residence.

Phratry: A grouping of two or more clans. A legend often "explains" why special links of rights and duties exist among particular clans. Phratries may be exogamous or endogamous or lack any marriage regulation.

Polyandry: A norm that allows a woman more than one husband. Few societies are polyandrous; the co-husbands are usually brothers.

Polygyny: A norm that allows a man more than one wife. Although the norms in many societies permit polygyny, it is common for the typical member to be monogamous. *See also* Sororal·polygyny.

Progeny price: Goods given to the wife's group at the time of marriage. The wealth transferred at the time of marriage is generally best understood as insuring that children will be a part of the groom's group. Originally, such practices were misinterpreted as a buying of wives, and the wealth was called a "bride price." *See also* Bride wealth.

Pseudo-kinship: Ties created between individuals that resemble kinship relations. These ties range in "strength" from stepparent to fraternity "brother."

Sororal polygyny: A norm that requires a second or later marriage to be with wife's sister. Parallel cousins and others are often in the category of "sister" to wife. *See also* Polygyny.

Unilateral cross-cousin marriage: An institution by which a man is expected to marry only the mother's brother's daughter (known as matrilateral cross-cousin marriage) or only the father's sister's daughter (known as patrilateral cross-cousin marriage). The former practice is far more common than the latter, and the debate over the reasons for its prevalence has been an important topic for social anthropology. *See also* Bilateral cross-cousin marriage.

Unilineal descent: A system that traces descent through only one sex. *See also* Cognatic descent.

Bibliography

Aberle, David, *et. al.*, 1963, "The Incest Taboo and the Mating Patterns of Animals," *American Anthropologist,* 65:253–265.

Barnes, J. A., 1962, "African Models in the New Guinea Highlands," *Man,* 62:5–9.

Barnett, H. G., 1960, *Being a Palauan.* New York: Holt, Rinehart and Winston, Inc.

Bascom, William, 1969, *The Yoruba of Southwestern Nigeria.* New York: Holt, Rinehart and Winston, Inc.

Basso, Keith, 1970, *The Cibecue Apache.* New York: Holt, Rinehart and Winston, Inc.

Beals, Alan, 1962, *Gopalpur: A South Indian Village.* New York: Holt, Rinehart and Winston, Inc.

Beattie, John, 1960, *Bunyoro: An African Kingdom.* New York: Holt, Rinehart and Winston, Inc.

Boissevain, Jeremy, 1969, *Hal-Farrug: A Village in Malta.* New York: Holt, Rinehart and Winston, Inc.

Chagnon, Napoleon, 1968, *Yąnomamö: The Fierce People.* New York: Holt, Rinehart and Winston, Inc.

DeVore, Irven (ed.), 1965, *Primate Behavior: Field Studies of Monkeys and Apes.* New York: Holt, Rinehart and Winston, Inc.

Dolhinow, Phyllis Jay (ed.), 1968, *Primates: Studies in Adaptation and Variability.* New York: Holt, Rinehart and Winston, Inc.

Dozier, Edward, 1966, *Hano: A Tewa Indian Community in Arizona.* New York: Holt, Rinehart and Winston, Inc.

————, 1967, *The Kalinga of Northern Luzon, Philippines.* New York: Holt, Rinehart and Winston, Inc.

————, 1970, *The Pueblo Indians of North America.* New York: Holt, Rinehart and Winston, Inc.

Eggan, Fred, 1950, *Social Organization of the Western Pueblos.* Chicago: University of Chicago Press.

Ekvall, Robert, 1968, *Fields on the Hoof: Nexus of Tibetan Nomadic Pastoralism.* New York: Holt, Rinehart and Winston, Inc.

Faron, Louis, 1968, *The Mapuche Indians of Chile.* New York: Holt, Rinehart and Winston, Inc.

Fortes, Meyer, 1953, "The Structure of Unilineal Descent Groups," *American Anthropologist,* 55:17–41.

Fox, Robin, 1967, *Kinship and Marriage.* Baltimore: Penguin Books.

Friedl, Ernestine, 1962, *Vasilika: A Village in Modern Greece.* New York: Holt, Rinehart and Winston, Inc.

Gamst, Frederick C., 1969, *The Qemant: A Pagan-Hebraic Peasantry of Ethiopia.* New York: Holt, Rinehart and Winston, Inc.

Goodenough, Ward, 1951, *Property, Kin and Community on Truk.* New Haven: Yale University Publications in Anthropology, No. 46.

Gough, Kathleen, 1962, "Nayar: Central and North," in *Matrilineal Kinship,* eds. David Schneider and Kathleen Gough. Berkeley: University of California Press.

Hart, C. W. M., and Arnold Pilling, 1960, *The Tiwi of North Australia.* New York: Holt, Rinehart and Winston, Inc.

Hudson, A. B., 1972, *Padju Epat: The Ma'anyan of Indonesian Borneo.* New York: Holt, Rinehart and Winston, Inc.

Leach, Edmund, 1954, *The Political Systems of Highland Burma.* London: London School of Economics and Political Science.

Lessa, William, 1966, *Ulithi: A Micronesian Design for Living.* New York: Holt, Rinehart and Winston, Inc.

Lewis, Oscar, 1960, *Tepoztlán: Village in Mexico.* New York: Holt, Rinehart and Winston, Inc.

Morgan, Lewis H., 1870, *Systems of Consanguinity and Affinity on the Human Family.* Washington, D.C.: Smithsonian Contributions to Knowledge, Vol. 17, No. 218.

Murdock, George (ed.), 1960, *Social Structure in Southeast Asia.* Chicago: Quadrangle Books.

Newman, Philip, 1965, *Knowing the Gururumba.* New York: Holt, Rinehart and Winston, Inc.

Norbeck, Edward, 1965. *Changing Japan.* New York: Holt, Rinehart and Winston, Inc.

Partridge, William, 1973, *The Hippie Ghetto: The Natural History of a Subculture.* New York: Holt, Rinehart and Winston, Inc.

Pospisil, Leopold, 1963, *The Kapauku Papuans of West New Guinea.* New York: Holt, Rinehart and Winston, Inc.

Richardson, Miles, 1970, *San Pedro, Columbia: Small Town in a Developing Society.* New York: Holt, Rinehart and Winston, Inc.

Schneider, David, 1965, "Some Muddles in the Models: Or, How the System Really Works," in *The Relevance of Models for Social Anthropology,* ed. M. Banton. New York: Praeger.

———, 1968, *American Kinship: A Cultural Account.* Englewood Cliffs, New Jersey: Prentice-Hall.

Schneider, David, and Kathleen Gough (eds.), 1962, *Matrilineal Kinship.* Berkeley: University of California Press.

Schneider, David, and George Homans, 1955, "Kinship Terminology and The American Kinship System," *American Anthropologist,* 57:1194–1208.

Schusky, Ernest L., 1972, *Manual for Kinship Analysis,* Second Edition. New York: Holt, Rinehart and Winston, Inc.

Slater, Mariam, 1959, "Ecological Factors in the Origin of Incest," *American Anthropologist,* 61:1042–1059.

Tiger, Lionel, and Robin Fox, 1971, *The Imperial Animal.* New York: Holt, Rinehart and Winston, Inc.

Trigger, Bruce, 1969, *The Huron: Farmers of the North.* New York: Holt, Rinehart and Winston, Inc.

Turner, Paul, 1972, *The Highland Chontal.* New York: Holt, Rinehart and Winston, Inc.

Uchendu, Victor, 1965, *The Igbo of Southeast Nigeria.* New York: Holt, Rinehart and Winston, Inc.

Vogt, Evon Z., 1970, *The Zinacantecos of Mexico: A Modern Maya Way of Life.* New York: Holt, Rinehart and Winston, Inc.

Williams, Thomas, 1965, *The Dusun: A North Borneo Society.* New York: Holt, Rinehart and Winston, Inc.